YORK NOTES

King Henry IV Part 1

William Shakespeare

Note by David Pinnington

 Longman   York Press

David Pinnington is hereby identified as author of this work in accordance with
Section 77 of the Copyright, Designs and Patents Act 1988

YORK PRESS
322 Old Brompton Road, London SW5 9JH

PEARSON EDUCATION LIMITED
Edinburgh Gate, Harlow,
Essex CM20 2JE, United Kingdom
Associated companies, branches and representatives throughout the world

First published 1999

ISBN 0–582–38233–5

Designed by Vicki Pacey
Illustrated by Chris Molan
Family trees by G.J. Galsworthy
Phototypeset by Gem Graphics, Trenance, Mawgan Porth, Cornwall
Colour reproduction and film output by Spectrum Colour
Produced by Addison Wesley Longman China Limited, Hong Kong

CONTENTS

PREFACE

York Notes are designed to give you a broader perspective on works of literature studied at GCSE and equivalent levels. We have carried out extensive research into the needs of the modern literature student prior to publishing this new edition. Our research showed that no existing series fully met students' requirements. Rather than present a single authoritative approach, we have provided alternative viewpoints, empowering students to reach their own interpretations of the text. York Notes provide a close examination of the work and include biographical and historical background, summaries, glossaries, analyses of characters, themes, structure and language, cultural connections and literary terms.

If you look at the Contents page you will see the structure for the series. However, there's no need to read from the beginning to the end as you would with a novel, play, poem or short story. Use the Notes in the way that suits you. Our aim is to help you with your understanding of the work, not to dictate how you should learn.

York Notes are written by English teachers and examiners, with an expert knowledge of the subject. They show you how to succeed in coursework and examination assignments, guiding you through the text and offering practical advice. Questions and comments will extend, test and reinforce your knowledge. Attractive colour design and illustrations improve clarity and understanding, making these Notes easy to use and handy for quick reference.

York Notes are ideal for:
- Essay writing
- Exam preparation
- Class discussion

The author of these notes is David Pinnington, who read English at the universities of York and Exeter, where he took an MA in Modern Fiction. He teaches in Devon and is a senior GCSE examiner for English and English Literature. He is the author of the York Notes on *Twelfth Night* and *The Tempest*.

The text used in these Notes is *King Henry IV Part 1* edited by A.R. Humphreys in the *Arden Shakespeare* series.

Health Warning: **This study guide will enhance your understanding, but should not replace the reading of the original text and/or study in class.**

PART ONE

INTRODUCTION

HOW TO STUDY A PLAY

You have bought this book because you wanted to study a play on your own. This may supplement classwork.

- Drama is a special 'kind' of writing (the technical term is 'genre') because it needs a performance in the theatre to arrive at a full interpretation of its meaning. When reading a play you have to imagine how it should be performed; the words alone will not be sufficient. Think of gestures and movements.

- Drama is always about conflict of some sort (it may be below the surface). Identify the conflicts in the play and you will be close to identifying the large ideas or themes which bind all the parts together.

- Make careful notes on themes, characters, plot and any sub-plots of the play.

- Playwrights find non-realistic ways of allowing an audience to see into the minds and motives of their characters. The 'soliloquy', in which a character speaks directly to the audience, is one such device. Does the play you are studying have any such passages?

- Which characters do you like or dislike in the play? Why? Do your sympathies change as you see more of these characters?

- Think of the playwright writing the play. Why were these particular arrangements of events, these particular sets of characters and these particular speeches chosen?

Studying on your own requires self-discipline and a carefully thought-out work plan in order to be effective. Good luck.

Family life

William Shakespeare was born at Stratford-upon-Avon in 1564. There is a record of his christening, 26 April, so we can assume he was born shortly before that date. His father, John Shakespeare, was a glove-maker and trader who later became high bailiff of Stratford; his mother, Mary Arden, was the daughter of a landowner. It is probable that William would have attended the local grammar school where the curriculum included Latin, rhetoric, logic and literature.

In 1582 Shakespeare married Anne Hathaway, a woman eight years older than himself, and their first child, Susanna, was christened in May 1583. In 1585 the twins Hamnet and Judith were born to Anne and William. Both Shakespeare's daughters lived to marry and have children, but Hamnet only lived until he was eleven – his burial took place in Stratford on 11 August, 1596.

Writing

Sometime after 1585 Shakespeare left Stratford and went to London where he became an actor and a dramatist. He worked first with a group of actors called Lord Pembroke's Men and later with a company called the Lord Chamberlain's Men (later the King's Men). His earliest plays, *Henry VI Parts 1–3*, *Richard III*, *Titus Andronicus* and the comedies *The Comedy of Errors*, *The Taming of the Shrew* and *The Two Gentlemen of Verona*, were performed around 1590–4. From the start Shakespeare was very successful in the theatre and his genius inspired the resentment of Robert Greene, a mediocre university-educated dramatist, who described the young playwright to his friends as 'an upstart Crow, beautified with our feathers'.

Henry IV Parts 1 and 2 belong to this period.

In the 1590s Shakespeare wrote six more comedies, culminating in *Twelfth Night* probably written in 1596–7. During this time he also wrote history plays, tragedies and the narrative poems, *Venus and Adonis* and

The Rape of Lucrece, in addition to the Sonnets which were published in 1609.

In the early years of the new century he turned his attention almost exclusively to **tragedy** and wrote some of the most powerful works in this **genre** (see Literary Terms) that have ever existed: *Hamlet* (1604–5), *Othello* (1604–5), *Macbeth* (1605–6), *King Lear* (1606–7) and *Antony and Cleopatra* (1606–7).

Although Shakespeare lived and worked for most of his life in London, he obviously did not forget Stratford. In 1596 he acquired the right to a coat of arms there, something his father had tried and failed to obtain, and in 1597 he bought New Place, a large house in the town. Later, in 1602, he acquired other property, and in about 1610 he returned to live permanently in Stratford.

Play-writing occupied Shakespeare until the final years of his life and between 1608–12 he produced the so-called 'last plays', *Pericles, Cymbeline, The Winter's Tale* and *The Tempest*. These plays suggest a mellowing in outlook and a concern for the relationships of parents and children, as if they were written by a man who was taking stock of his life and thinking of the generation that would replace him.

Shakespeare wrote a will in January 1616, and died barely three months later on 23 April. He left bequests to Stratford acquaintances and to his actor friends, Burbage, Heminges and Condell. The last two edited the first complete edition of Shakespeare's works, the First Folio of 1623.

CONTEXT & SETTING

Historical perspective

In 1399 there was a crisis in English national life when Henry Bolingbroke, Duke of Lancaster, deposed

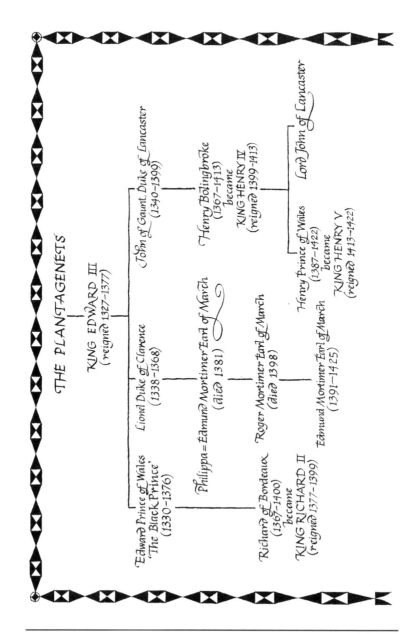

THE PLANTAGENETS

KING EDWARD III
(reigned 1327–1377)

Edward Prince of Wales
'The Black Prince'
(1330–1376)

Lionel Duke of Clarence
(1338–1368)

John of Gaunt, Duke of Lancaster
(1340–1399)

Richard of Bordeaux
(1367–1400)
became
KING RICHARD II
(reigned 1377–1399)

Philippa = Edmund Mortimer Earl of March
(died 1381)

Henry Bolingbroke
(1367–1413)
became
KING HENRY IV
(reigned 1399–1413)

Lord John of Lancaster

Roger Mortimer Earl of March
(died 1398)

Henry Prince of Wales
(1387–1422)
became
KING HENRY V
(reigned 1413–1422)

Edmund Mortimer Earl of March
(1391–1425)

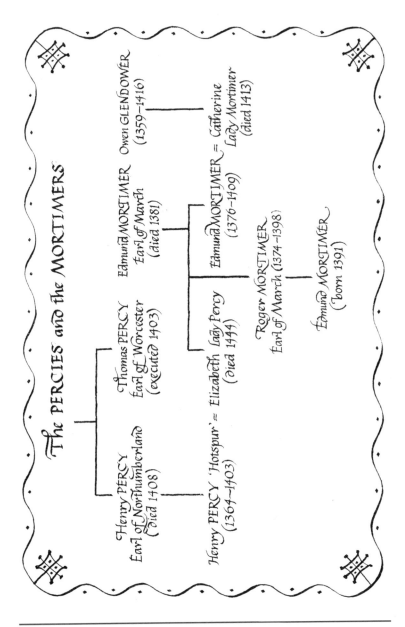

The PERCIES and the MORTIMERS

Henry PERCY
Earl of Northumberland
(died 1408)

Thomas PERCY
Earl of Worcester
(executed 1403)

Edmund MORTIMER
Earl of March
(died 1381)

Owen GLENDOWER
(1359–1416)

Henry PERCY 'Hotspur' = Elizabeth Lady Percy
(1364–1403)   (died 1444)

Roger MORTIMER
Earl of March (1374–1398)

Edmund MORTIMER = Catherine
(1376–1409)   Lady Mortimer
                              (died 1413)

Edmund MORTIMER
(born 1391)

*The action of
Henry IV, Part 1
takes place
between the battle
of Holmedon, 14
September 1402,
and the battle of
Shrewsbury, 21
July 1403.*

King Richard II and usurped his crown. Bolingbroke had been banished from England by Richard who then confiscated his lands and his title. When he returned to England to reclaim what Richard had taken from him, Bolingbroke enrolled the help of the powerful Percy family in Northumberland. As he acquired more supporters in England he became more ambitious and more powerful, so that he was able to turn his back on the Percys and achieve the throne.

Shakespeare was fascinated by Bolingbroke's usurpation and wrote eight plays on the historical events that followed it (see below), but he was not interested in using the theatre merely to transmit historical facts. In his search for emotional and intellectual truth he leaves out much that a historian would consider important. He invents details and characters (such as Falstaff), and changes some of the facts to achieve the dramatic effect he requires.

Shakespeare took the historical events from the *Chronicles of England* by Ralph Holinshed. Here are some of the alterations he made:

- In Holinshed, Glendower is depicted as a predatory outlaw, but in the play Shakespeare turns him into a civilised poet-scholar, with musical gifts.
- Hotspur is made the same age as Prince Hal, when in reality he was thirty-nine at the time of the battle of Shrewsbury and the prince was fifteen.
- Hotspur was not killed by Prince Hal at Shrewsbury.
- King Henry IV planned his crusade at the end of his life, with the intention of uniting Europe against the infidel, and not, as Shakespeare implies, in expiation of his sin in usurping Richard.
- There were, in fact, two Edmund Mortimers at the time, one was the child heir to the throne and the other was his uncle, who married Glendower's daughter.

- Shakespeare follows Holinshed in confusing two rebellions. The 'indenture tripartite' which the rebels argue over in Act III, Scene 1, belongs to the year 1405, two years after the setting of the play.
- At the end the king is made to seem more merciful than he was in reality: Hotspur's body was crushed between two millstones, and then beheaded and quartered.

The history plays

Shakespeare's eight history plays, which were inspired by Bolingbroke's usurpation of Richard II in 1399, make up two tetralogies, that is, two groups of four plays. Shakespeare did not write them in the order of the reigns which they describe. The first group he composed consists of the three Henry VI plays and Richard III; the second group begins with Richard II, followed by both parts of Henry IV, and ends with Henry V.

The orthodox view of these eight plays is that they demonstrate how wrong it was for Bolingbroke to rebel against the king whom it was believed had been appointed by God to rule. In *Henry V*, when Prince Hal is king, he is aware of the possibility of God's punishment as he is about to fight the battle of Agincourt: 'Not today, O'Lord! / O not today, think not upon the fault / My father made in compassing the crown!' Henry V is spared retribution, but during the reigns of Henry VI and Richard III England endured much suffering. It was believed that with the accession of Henry Tudor (King Henry VII) in 1485, the country finally achieved peace and unity.

Shakespeare's audience

The Elizabethan audience for whom Shakespeare wrote his history plays lived in a time of political uncertainty. Queen Elizabeth's right to the throne was being challenged by the Roman Catholics and her supporters had good reason to propagate the myth that the rule of the queen or king of England was divinely sanctioned by God, and that to rebel against it was a sin. Her grandfather, Henry Tudor (Henry VII), had resolved the historical disputes which had originated in Bolingbroke's usurpation by uniting the houses of York (Mortimer's descendants) and Lancaster (Bolingbroke's descent). Shakespeare was dependent for patronage on Elizabeth's court so it is understandable that his dramatisation of English history should reflect the way the Tudors wanted to see themselves. The final play, *Henry V*, shows Prince Hal as a national hero, defeating the French at Agincourt, and does not discuss the issues raised by his father's usurpation. However, Shakespeare did not have a simple view of anything; his mind was too imaginative and sceptical to be constricted by a simplistic orthodoxy such as nationalism, or the assumption of the divine right of kings. Taken as a whole, the history plays reveal his ability to weave a multitude of viewpoints into a vast, complex tapestry of drama.

Part two

Summaries

General summary

Act I

The Palace of Westminster. King Henry rules a country temporarily at peace. He is anxious to unite the opposing factions within his realm against a common enemy and plans a crusade to the Holy Land to fight the pagan Turks. In doing this the king hopes to atone for the way he gained the throne of England: as Henry Bolingbroke he returned from exile and deposed Richard II, usurping the throne and causing his death. When the play opens King Henry has been planning the crusade for a year. But his hopes are frustrated. The Earl of Westmoreland [sic] brings news that Mortimer has been defeated and captured by the Welsh, while in the north 'the gallant Hotspur', Harry Percy, has fought and won a bloody battle with the Scots. Hotspur has taken many prisoners, but will only give up one. King Henry is impressed by Hotspur's fighting spirit, and he compares him favourably to his own dissolute son, Henry, Prince of Wales. However, the king postpones his crusade to Jerusalem and sends for Hotspur to answer for his 'pride' in withholding the prisoners, who rightfully belong to him.

The apartment of the Prince of Wales, London. Prince Hal and Sir John Falstaff are chatting, their talk full of witty, teasing word-play. Eventually, Poins enters and proposes they rob some travellers on the road between Canterbury and London. Prince Hal refuses to join them, but after Sir John has left, Poins confides to the prince a counter-plot, the purpose of which is to make a fool of Falstaff: they will let the knight and his accomplices carry out the robbery without them and then, in disguise, they will rob him

of his spoils. Alone on the stage, Prince Hal in a
soliloquy (see Literary Terms) reveals his true thoughts
to the audience. He knows that, as heir to the throne,
these friends of his are unsuitable. He will go along
with their wild schemes for the time being, but
eventually he will 'throw off' this 'loose behaviour' and
reform. He will do it in such a way that people will
admire him for rising above his reputation for wasteful
idleness.

The council chamber, Windsor. Hotspur and his
father, the Earl of Northumberland, together with
the Earl of Worcester, have arrived to be confronted
by the resentful king, who reminds them of their
allegiance to him. Worcester angers King Henry by
pointing out that it was the Percy family that helped
him achieve the throne. But Northumberland and his
son, Hotspur, are more placatory. They claim that the
report of their denial of prisoners has been exaggerated
and maliciously distorted. The king insists that the
prisoners be handed over without any conditions
and he vehemently refuses to pay a ransom for
Mortimer, the Earl of March, captured by the Welsh.
Hotspur speaks in defence of the earl, whom Henry
has accused of being a traitor. When the king has
gone, Worcester and Northumberland inform Hotspur
that Richard II proclaimed Mortimer his true heir.
Hotspur is incensed. His sense of honour is affronted
by the way his family has helped put 'this canker
Bolingbroke' upon the throne of England. When
he calms down, his uncle reveals a plot to oppose
the king and Hotspur gladly agrees to play his part
in it.

Act II   An inn yard, Rochester. In the early hours of the
morning two carriers get ready for another day's work.
Gadshill appears and talks to the inn's chamberlain,
who confirms the presence of two wealthy travellers in

the inn. It is clear they are to be the victims of the projected robbery.

The highway at Gad's Hill. The robbers meet and Prince Hal and Poins play their trick on Falstaff, who is angry at the start of the scene because Poins has taken his horse. After they have robbed the travellers, the thieves are set upon by Hal and Poins; leaving their plunder behind, they quickly run away in confusion, to the delight of the tricksters.

Warkworth castle, Northumberland. Hotspur is reading a letter from an unidentified nobleman who is reluctant to join the rebels. The letter warns of the danger of such an undertaking. Hotspur is contemptuous of the writer's fears and certain that he is the sort of person who will betray the rebels. He is joined by his wife, Kate, who complains that he has been neglecting her and tries to find out what has been worrying him so much recently. Hotspur is too preoccupied with his plans to answer Kate directly. He tells her he is leaving, but that she will shortly follow him.

The Boar's Head tavern, Eastcheap. Prince Hal has been drinking with the inn's servants and summons Poins to watch him play a trick on one of them. It is a clumsy prank and Poins has difficulty understanding it. Eventually, Falstaff arrives, cursing all the cowards in the world and deliberately ignoring the prince. He soon accuses Hal and Poins of cowardice, for running away from the robbery, and then proceeds to give a fictitious and contradictory account of it until Hal confronts him with what really happened. Falstaff claims he knew the attackers were Hal and Poins and that he ran away 'on instinct', because he could not kill the heir to the throne. Suddenly, a messenger arrives with news of the rebellion and a summons for Hal to go to his father, the king. Knowing he will have to answer for his irresponsible conduct, Hal decides to practise what he will say in a mock interview, with Falstaff playing the part of the king. After reprimanding Hal for the bad company he keeps, Falstaff singles himself out as the young prince's only virtuous friend. Hal then takes the part of the king. He violently condemns Falstaff as a 'misleader of youth' and the old knight replies with a defence of himself. Finally, the sheriff arrives searching for the robbers. While Falstaff hides behind a curtain, the prince promises to make his friend accountable for his crimes. After the sheriff has left, Falstaff is discovered asleep and the prince announces that he will repay with interest what the travellers have lost.

Act III   The archdeacon's house, Bangor. The leaders of the rebellion gather to make their plans. Owen Glendower is mocked by Hotspur for claiming to have magical powers. When they plan to divide England and Wales into three parts, ruled by Mortimer, Glendower and Hotspur respectively, the latter protests that his part is too small. After first refusing to have the division of land altered, Glendower gives in to Hotspur and goes off in search of the ladies, to tell them of Mortimer's and Hotspur's departure for Shrewsbury. While he is gone, Mortimer and Worcester reprimand Hotspur for his rudeness to Glendower. There is a final gathering with music and singing in which Glendower's Welsh-speaking daughter, who has married Mortimer, bids a tearful farewell to her husband; and Hotspur teasingly parts from his Kate.

The palace, London. The interview takes place between King Henry and the Prince of Wales. The king feels that God is punishing him for his former 'mistreadings' by having a son who is so dissolute and irresponsible. Hal admits his faults and asks for forgiveness. After describing his own conduct before he came to the throne, the king compares Prince Hal's present behaviour to that of Richard II, who 'mingled his royalty with capering fools' and was not respected by the people. He implies Hotspur commands more respect than Prince Hal. The prince promises to redeem his lost reputation and fight nobly for this father. The king decides to trust his son and makes plans for the forthcoming battle with the rebels.

The Boar's Head tavern, Eastcheap. Falstaff has a hangover and vows to repent. Bardolph mocks his fatness and in return Falstaff ridicules Bardolph for his red face. After an argument with the Hostess, Prince Hal enters with Peto. Falstaff has claimed that valuable items were picked from his pocket while he was asleep; the prince admits that he picked Falstaff's pockets and that there was nothing there worth having. Falstaff apologises to the Hostess and Prince Hal informs Falstaff that he is to lead a company of infantry against Percy.

Act IV   The rebel camp, Shrewsbury. Hotspur is pleased to have the brave Douglas, a former enemy, fighting on his side, but soon receives news which casts a shadow over his venture. His father, the Earl of Northumberland, sends word that he is sick and cannot join the rebels. He also learns something of the great strength of the king's approaching army, and is told that Glendower's force is unable to join his own.

A public road near Coventry. Falstaff is leading his company of foot soldiers to Shrewsbury. He admits to using the king's authority to conscript only those who were able to buy out their services, that is, to bribe Falstaff not to take them to war. All he has left is a wretched band of ragged misfits. When Prince Hal sees them he calls them 'pitiful rascals', but Sir John assures him that they are good enough to die in a war.

The rebel camp, Shrewsbury. Sir Walter Blunt interrupts an argument among the rebels with an offer of peace from the king. To Henry's request for a statement of their grievances, Hotspur replies with an account of how the Percy family helped him to the throne and how he has subsequently betrayed his promises. Hotspur assures Blunt that he will send a formal reply to the king the next day.

The archbishop's palace, York. Fearful that the weakened rebel force will lose against the king, the Archbishop of York sends letters to other members of the confederacy of rebels, advising them to prepare for future conflict.

Act V

The king's camp, Shrewsbury. Worcester arrives and King Henry makes a final offer of peace. The rebels' grievances are repeated and Prince Hal offers to fight Hotspur in single combat in order to avoid widespread bloodshed. Worcester returns to the rebels with the king's peace offer, but neither Prince Hal nor the king believe it will be accepted. They prepare for battle, leaving Falstaff alone contemplating the nature of 'honour'.

The rebel camp, Shrewsbury. Worcester arrives back from the king's camp and decides not to tell Hotspur of the offer of peace. He believes Henry will go back on his promise to forgive the rebels and that he and Northumberland, in particular, will be punished for their part in the rebellion. He tells Hotspur that the king wishes to do battle. He does, however, convey the prince's personal challenge to Hotspur, with Vernon relating how modestly Hal had spoken this challenge. Hotspur promises to kill the prince during the battle, and the rebels prepare to fight.

The field of battle, Shrewsbury. The battle has begun in earnest and Sir Walter Blunt, disguised as the king, is killed by Douglas. Falstaff appears, boasting that he has led his soldiers to slaughter and telling Prince Hal that he has killed Hotspur. The prince informs him that Percy is 'living to kill thee'. Soon the king appears with both his sons, who have been bravely fighting. Although wounded, Prince Hal sees off Douglas when he attacks his father. Eventually Hotspur and Prince Hal confront each other and fight. The prince kills Hotspur and pronounces a tribute to his bravery. As he walks away he notices Falstaff lying on the ground pretending to be dead after an encounter with Douglas. The prince mourns his friend briefly then departs, and Falstaff stands up. He congratulates himself on saving his own life through 'discretion' and decides to claim it was he who killed Hotspur. He stabs the corpse in the thigh and when Prince Hal and his brother return, tries to make them believe that Hotspur had only been wounded, like himself, and that they had both recovered at the same time and had fought for an hour until Falstaff had killed the knight. Prince Hal is amused by this 'lie' and promises to let Falstaff take the credit for Hotspur's death.

The play ends with Henry IV confronting the rebels. Worcester is condemned to death and Douglas is pardoned by Prince Hal on account of his brave deeds in battle. The king sends his son, John of Lancaster, to York, to meet the rebel force of Northumberland, and he and Prince Hal set off for Wales to fight the forces of Glendower and Mortimer.

Detailed Summaries

ACT I

SCENE 1

A crusade would be a good reason to raise an army devoted to the king.

King Henry IV is addressing members of his court. He speaks of the civil conflicts which have beset the country since he usurped the throne from Richard II. In the hope of uniting his people in the fragile peace that has been achieved, he had decided to embark upon a crusade to the Holy Land. However, the previous evening his council had learnt that Mortimer, Earl of March, who had been defending the English/Welsh border from a Welsh uprising, had been defeated and captured by the Welsh. This, together with the news that Hotspur has been engaged in fighting with the Scots in the north, has caused the postponement of the crusade. Hotspur has fought bravely and has taken many prisoners. When Westmoreland remarks that a prince would be proud of such conquests, the king is reminded of his son, Henry, Prince of Wales. He speaks enviously of Lord Northumberland, Hotspur's father, and wishes he had Harry (Hotspur) Percy for a son instead of the wild and irresponsible Prince Hal.

If nobles were captured in battle, their ransom belonged to the king.

Hotspur, however, will only give up one of the prisoners to the king. Westmoreland believes this proud defiance shows the evil influence of Hotspur's uncle, the Earl of Worcester. The king sends for Hotspur to explain his actions.

COMMENT

King Henry is afflicted with many problems.

The king's opening speech provides a vivid picture of the evils of civil war. Henry's **personification** (see Literary Terms) of England as a mother daubed 'with her own children's blood' (line 6), is an expression of the familiar Elizabethan equation between the human body and the body politic. He also compares the civil fighting to disruptive meteors (line 10), which again indicates another Elizabethan correspondence: that the universe was capable of reflecting important events through storms, lightning, shooting stars and so on. This notion is used several times during the play.

Notice the heavy flatness in the rhythm of this speech. Henry is tired and well aware that this 'frighted peace' (line 2) is only temporary. Even as he speaks of the projected crusade he must know that it cannot take place until he has quelled all the forces of rebellion within his country.

Through Westmoreland's speeches we gain a glimpse of the king's enemies in the play: the 'irregular and wild Glendower' (line 40) and the 'gallant Hotspur' (line 52). *The theme of honour is associated with Hotspur, but is qualified by his 'pride'.* And a deliberate parallel is created between the latter and the king's son and heir, Prince Hal. This will be sustained throughout the play. By making Hotspur and Hal the same age, Shakespeare invites the audience to reflect on the issue of rightful inheritance and to compare the qualities of the two Harrys.

The scene ends with an assertion of Henry's authority – the Percys are summoned to Windsor.

GLOSSARY

2   **pant** breathing space

11   **one nature … one substance** fellow countrymen

21   **impressed** enlisted

36   **athwart** cross purposes

69   **Balk'd** piled up

88   **Plantagenet** surname of the English royal family, 1154–1485

97   **prune** trim

SCENE *2*

Prince Hal and Sir John Falstaff are engaged in witty bantering conversation at the prince's London apartment. Their jokes are about the irresponsible lifestyle they are following, of Falstaff's drinking and gluttony, of thieving and its possible consequences. *The prince's friends plan mischief.* Eventually, just as Poins, another of their friends enters, a robbery is proposed. Poins tells them that early the next morning some rich travellers will be on the road between Canterbury and London. He and another friend, Gadshill, have set it all up. The robbery will be easy, and by the next evening they will all be having supper in Eastcheap with their purses full of crowns.

The prince refuses to take part in the illegal action, and Falstaff berates him for his timidity, but Poins asks the knight to leave him alone with the prince so that he can persuade him to take part in the adventure.

Falstaff's lies will be shown up.

When Falstaff has left, Poins reveals a secret plan, the purpose of which is to make a fool of Falstaff by 'the incomprehensible lies' (line 181) he will tell when they all meet up at supper time. Poins's plan is to let Falstaff, Bardolph, Peto and Gadshill carry out the robbery without them, then to set upon them and take their spoils. The prince agrees to take part and Poins leaves to make the arrangements.

The prince expresses his real views.

Left alone on the stage, Prince Hal speaks his thoughts to the audience in a **soliloquy** (see Literary Terms). He says he has no illusions about the kind of people he is mixing with. He is like the sun surrounded by 'base contagious clouds' (line 193). Soon, however, he will show himself as he really is and reform, throwing off 'this loose behaviour' (line 203) in such a way that people will admire him for transcending his faults.

COMMENT

The scene provides a vivid contrast to the previous one.

We meet Prince Hal and his best friend, Sir John Falstaff. At the start of the comic **sub-plot** (see Literary Terms) we discover what the king meant by 'riot and dishonour' (I.1.84): Prince Hal's friend is a thief and a drunkard.

Hal gives the audience a picture of Falstaff's lifestyle.

The opening conversation is rich in word-play, quips and quiddities, as Falstaff describes Hal's talk (line 44), and is a kind of contest between the two characters. Falstaff may be suffering from a hangover, but his mind is sharp and creative. His **puns** and **allusions** (see Literary Terms) turn the conversation in unexpected directions.

Falstaff makes several playful references to Prince Hal's status as heir to the throne, thus serving to anticipate Hal's reformation later in the play. Also, the prince detaches himself from the values associated with Falstaff when he refuses to take part in the robbery, and this detachment becomes explicit in his final **soliloquy** (see Literary Terms). He is not ready to reject the irresponsible life just yet, but his sense of personal destiny is powerfully expressed. The image of the sun 'breaking through the foul and ugly mists' (line 197) is intended to make an indelible impression upon the mind of the audience.

The scene ends seriously with Hal's verse soliloquy

GLOSSARY

13	**come near me**	'You've got me there'
15	**Phoebus**	Greek sun god
41	**old lad of the castle**	a pun on 'Oldcastle'. Sir John Oldcastle (d.1417) was the original Falstaff
43	**quips**	clever replies
44	**quiddities**	quibbles
66	**jumps**	agrees
80	**vanity**	empty waste of time
98	**baffle me**	shame
119	**cozening**	cheating
124	**vizards**	masks
181	**incomprehensible**	boundless
191	**unyoked**	without restraint
	humour	mood
204	**the debt I never promised**	the responsibility which my early life showed no promise of

SCENE 3

Another set of characters is introduced.

In the council chamber at Windsor the king confronts Worcester, Northumberland and Hotspur. He says he has not been treated with the respect due to him as a king and is angered when Worcester reminds him that it was the Percy family who helped him achieve the

*Hotspur's vivid
description of the
emissary brings
some humour to
the scene.*

throne. Almost immediately, Worcester is identified
with 'danger and disobedience' (line 15). For such bold
speaking, Worcester is dismissed from the chamber.
Northumberland and his son, Hotspur, then try to
appease the king. They claim that Henry has been
misled by inaccurate reports of Hotspur's refusal to
surrender his prisoners: it was not done with a
calculated desire to disobey the king, but under the
pressure of difficult circumstances. King Henry remains
dissatisfied. He is especially angry because Hotspur
continues to deny him the prisoners and will only give
them up when the king agrees to ransom the captured
Mortimer. This Henry will never do; he regards Mortimer
as a traitor, who has betrayed the lives of his soldiers in
the battle against the Welsh and has now married the
daughter of Owen Glendower, the king's enemy.

Hotspur is enraged at this accusation and speaks
passionately in Mortimer's defence, describing him as a
courageous soldier who fought loyally against
Glendower. The angry king calls Hotspur a liar and
leaves the stage threatening punishment unless the
prisoners are sent to him.

Worcester returns and explains that Henry's refusal to
ransom Mortimer is due to the fact that King Richard

proclaimed him next in line to the throne. When he learns this, Hotspur expresses great shame at the part his own family has played in setting 'this canker Bolingbroke' (line 174) upon the throne of England. Eventually, his uncle and father manage to calm him down and Worcester unfolds a plot to oppose the king. With the help of the Earl of Douglas, the Archbishop of York and Glendower they will raise an army strong enough to overthrow King Henry. Hotspur is more than willing to join them.

At the end of the scene the plot against King Henry is set in motion.

C OMMENT

In this scene we are provided with information about the grievances of the rebels. We learn of the resentment felt by the Percy family who had helped Henry Bolingbroke on his return from exile. More importantly, we hear of the 'fault' which lies in Henry's usurpation of the throne from Richard II. The Percy family had helped Bolingbroke regain the property which Richard confiscated, but on acquiring his rightful heritage, the duchy of Lancaster, Bolingbroke became ambitious for the crown.

Clearly the king feels guilty. He is suspicious of Worcester in particular and recognises the Earl's 'dangerous' state of mind. It is Worcester who has devised the plot to oppose Henry, and who understands why he so adamantly refuses to ransom Mortimer. As the legitimate heir to the throne, proclaimed by Richard II, Mortimer is a real threat to Henry's authority.

Compare the presentation of Hotspur in this scene with Prince Hal in the previous one.

This is the first appearance of Hotspur and true to his nickname he shows himself to be fiery and impulsive. His wordy speeches on battle and honour reveal a man who gives himself away too easily. He is courageously devoted to fighting – to 'fields, and blows, and groans' (line 296) – but lacks the political skill to pause and dissemble. Notice the contempt this honest man of action has for 'politician Bolingbroke' (line 238). In

Elizabethan times the word 'politician' was almost invariably equated with hypocrisy and cunning.

By the end of Act I both main **plot** and **sub-plot** (see Literary Terms) have been set in motion. The exposition demonstrates Shakespeare's theatrical skill in raising audience expectations and anticipating future events. It is likely that at this stage sympathy will be with the rebels because Henry achieved the throne by illegitimate means. However, he is presented as a king anxious to make amends for his faults and rule a united country. Are the rebels justified in plunging the realm into a civil conflict in which many lives will be lost?

GLOSSARY		
6	**condition**	natural disposition
26	**misprision**	misunderstanding
44	**holiday**	affected
86	**indent with fears**	make an agreement with cowards
134	**ingrate**	ungrateful
237	**pismires**	ants
244	**Ravenspurgh**	town on Yorkshire coast where Bolingbroke returned from exile
278	**head**	armed force

A *Identify the speaker.*

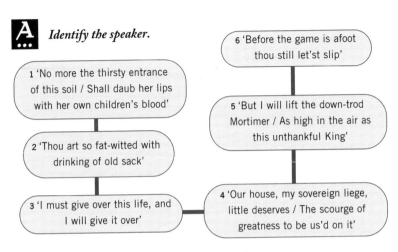

1 'No more the thirsty entrance of this soil / Shall daub her lips with her own children's blood'

2 'Thou art so fat-witted with drinking of old sack'

3 'I must give over this life, and I will give it over'

4 'Our house, my sovereign liege, little deserves / The scourge of greatness to be us'd on it'

5 'But I will lift the down-trod Mortimer / As high in the air as this unthankful King'

6 'Before the game is afoot thou still let'st slip'

Identify the person 'to whom' this comment refers.

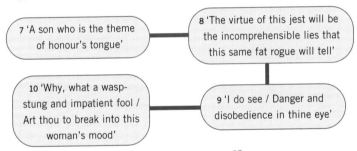

7 'A son who is the theme of honour's tongue'

8 'The virtue of this jest will be the incomprehensible lies that this same fat rogue will tell'

9 'I do see / Danger and disobedience in thine eye'

10 'Why, what a wasp-stung and impatient fool / Art thou to break into this woman's mood'

Check your answers on page 85.

B *Consider these issues.*

a How we are given some insight into King Henry's political skills in the opening scene

b How we learn something about the rebels before they appear on stage.

c The way the characters of Prince Harry and Harry Percy are contrasted, and why.

d The ways Shakespeare has established the main plot and the sub-plot by the end of the act.

e The relationship between Falstaff and Prince Hal.

f The way important historical information is given.

ACT II

SCENE 1 In the early hours of the morning two carriers are seen getting ready for their day's work. They shout for the inn's ostler to bring their horses and they complain about the flea-ridden accommodation. Gadshill enters and speaks with a chamberlain who has given him information about a rich franklin and an auditor who are staying at the inn. These will be the victims of the robbery and Gadshill promises to pay his informant with a share of the plunder.

COMMENT

The price of oats trebled between 1593 and 1596.

This short scene provides a realistic 'bridge' between the previous act and the robbery. It is rich in evocative detail. The condition of the horses and the slowness of the ostler to respond, the complaints about the new management of the inn, the insanitary custom of urinating into the fireplace, the details of the carrier's cargoes – all testify to Shakespeare's keen observation of ordinary experience.

Gadshill's humorous account of thieves and thieving anticipates the robbery.

Through the conversation between Gadshill and the chamberlain we hear about the different types of thieves who were active in Elizabethan England, the 'foot-landrakers' (line 72) and the 'long-staff sixpenny strikers' (line 73). With delicious **irony** (see Literary Terms), Gadshill says that his gang has none of these low-life criminals in it, but is made up of a much better class of person, including accountants ('great onyers', line 75).

GLOSSARY

2 **Charles' wain** the constellation of stars known as the Plough or Great Bear
52 **holds current** it is still true
53 **franklin** free-born landowner
60 **Saint Nicholas** patron saint of, among others, travellers and thieves. Hence 'Saint Nicholas' clerks' means 'highwaymen'
68 **Trojans** good companions

SCENE *2*

On the highway at Gad's Hill the robbers assemble to carry out their plan. Poins plays a trick on Falstaff by hiding his horse. The knight's comical outrage is interrupted by Gadshill and Bardolph, who warn of the approach of the rich travellers. Prince Hal and Poins go off as planned, leaving Falstaff and his gang to carry out the robbery. After this is done, the prince and Poins return in disguise to rob the thieves. The gang puts up little resistance and Hal and Poins are highly amused at their terror and confusion.

COMMENT

Much comic business is made out of Falstaff's size and breathlessness.

The comedy in this scene largely centres around Falstaff. Although he does not know about the planned trick, he seems to be sharing it with the audience: 'A plague upon it when thieves cannot be true one to another' (lines 27–8). When the travellers arrive he is more talk than action, urging the gang to 'cut the villains' throats' (line 80) and afterwards cursing Hal and Poins for their apparent cowardice.

Notice the way Shakespeare reminds the audience of Hal's status and lineage through Falstaff's words in lines 39, 40, 42 and 64. These references and the trick that is played on Falstaff serve the developing sense of Hal's disengagement from Falstaff's world.

The scene ends with the audience anticipating further comedy when Falstaff discovers how he has been tricked.

GLOSSARY

    2   **gummed** starched
  12   **squier** measure
  51   **Case ye** put on your masks
  84   **gorbellied** big bellied
  85   **chuffs** often applied to rich citizens

SCENE *3*

Hotspur is in his castle reading a letter from a lord who knows about the plot to oppose King Henry. The writer claims sympathy with the rebels' cause, but warns

The letter alerts the Hotspur of the dangers involved. He claims Hotspur's
audience to the friends are untested, that the time is wrong for a
dangers of rebellion. rebellion and that the 'plot' is altogether too weak. For
these reasons he will not be joining the rebels. Hotspur
is contemptuous of the man and curses himself for
inviting such a coward to take part in 'so honourable an
action' (line 34).

Kate's description Hotspur's wife, Kate, enters and proceeds to scold her
of Hotspur reveals husband for neglecting her. She wants to know why he
a man obsessed has been so distracted and depressed recently. Hotspur
with war. ignores her and sends a servant off to get his horse
ready. Kate persists and Hotspur softens towards her,
explaining that the time is not right for love-making.
He will love her 'infinitely' (line 104) when he is on his
war-horse, and though he loves and trusts her above all
others, she is still a woman and therefore cannot keep a
secret. What he can tell her is that, wherever he goes
today, she will shortly follow.

C OMMENT

Kate provides us with some insight into another aspect
of Hotspur's character and through this we are made
Compare the more aware of the seriousness of the situation. Hotspur
picture of Hotspur is clearly more worried about the enterprise than his
in this scene with vigorous dismissal of the letter-writer's fears would
that given by Hal indicate.
in the next,
II.4.99–106. The fact that Hotspur has passed on details about the
rebellion to someone who cannot be trusted confirms
the view of his character given in Act I, Scene 3, that
he is impulsive and indiscreet. But not so indiscreet that
he will confide in a woman!

The insertion of this scene after the robbery gives the
illusion of time passing, during which Prince Hal and
Poins will have made their way back to the tavern.

GLOSSARY

    12 **unsorted** badly chosen

    32 **go to buffets** 'kick myself'

52   **retires** retreats
53   **palisadoes** defence of stakes in the grounds
54   **basilisks** heavy artillery
      culverin small canon
63   **hest** command
73   **Esperance** Hope; motto of the Percy family
86   **paraquito** parrot
93   **mammets** dolls

SCENE 4

Only very special guests would be invited down to drink in the cellar.

At the Boar's Head tavern in Eastcheap Prince Hal has been fraternising with the servants. He is pleased to be on first-name terms with some of these 'drawers' and tells Poins that they approve of him far more than 'proud' Jack Falstaff. One of the servants he finds particularly amusing, and to pass the time before Falstaff arrives, he decides to play a trick on this slow-witted boy.

Hal depicts Hotspur as a homicidal maniac.

The trick is neither very clever nor funny, and Poins, who has participated in it, asks Hal what the point was. The prince replies that he is in the mood to indulge in anything, but is 'not yet of Percy's mind' (line 99).

Suddenly, Falstaff and the gang of robbers burst in, with Falstaff cursing all cowards and pointedly ignoring the prince. He eventually accuses Hal and Poins outright for running away from the robbery and not backing up their friends. He then describes how the loot was taken from them by 'a hundred upon poor four of us' (lines 159–60). Egged on by the prince, Falstaff's lies become more and more inconsistent until he contradicts himself once too often. Hal asks how he could have known that his fierce attackers were dressed in 'Kendal green' if it was so dark he could not see his hand. Falstaff refuses to answer; even it he were forced

The prince was very thin and tall, hence Falstaff's choice of insults (line 240 ff).

to do so, he says, he would not give a reason. So Hal tells him plainly what happened: how, after watching the four robbers set on the four travellers, Hal and Poins attacked the robbers, took their loot, and sent them packing, with Falstaff running off crying for mercy like a bull-calf.

Sir John is not at all put out by this, indeed he has probably already sensed he has been tricked, and he explains that he ran off in such a cowardly way 'on instinct' (line 269). He knew all the time it was Hal and Poins attacking them: could he have killed the heir to the throne?

A messenger arrives from the king, summoning Prince Hal to court. The revellers learn of the impending rebellion and Falstaff tells Hal that he will be 'horribly chid' (line 368) by his father when he sees him in the morning. He suggests they practise what he is going to say. A mock interview ensues, with Falstaff at first playing the part of the king.

'King' Falstaff condemns Prince Hal's behaviour.

The interview starts off with the 'king' reprimanding Hal for his irresponsible behaviour and unsuitable friends: 'Shall the son of England prove a thief, and take purses?' (lines 404–5). But one friend is singled out for extensive praise, 'A goodly portly man', namely Falstaff himself, whom Hal is urged to keep while the rest should be banished. The prince then 'deposes' his 'father' and takes the part of the king, while Falstaff plays Hal. The 'king' accuses 'Hal' of being 'violently

Falstaff, 'Prince of Wales', commends his real self.

carried away from grace' (lines 440–1) by Falstaff, who he describes as a 'misleader of youth' (line 456). Still in his role as Hal, Falstaff defends himself eloquently. All Hal's friends may be banished, but not Jack Falstaff, 'banish plump Jack, and banish all the world' (lines 473–4). The prince replies that he will.

The scene ends with the arrival of the sheriff, come to apprehend Falstaff for the Gad's Hill robbery. Falstaff conceals himself behind a curtain, where he falls asleep while Prince Hal promises the sheriff that he will make his friend answer for his crimes on the following day. Hal also promises to repay all the stolen money, with interest.

COMMENT

The Falstaffian comedy is now integrated into the play as a whole.

Prince Hal's cruel streak.

The comic **sub-plot** comes to a head in this long scene and is interwoven with the main **plot** (see Literary Terms) when Hal is summoned to court and he and his friends hear of the rebellion (lines 330–56).

At the start of the scene Hal is shown to have the 'common touch' through his account of his drinking session in the cellar with the servants. This could be seen as a good quality in a Prince of Wales. However, the joke against the inarticulate and harassed Francis seems cruel and patronising to modern audiences. To the Elizabethans, 'gulling' was a commonplace feature of their theatrical entertainments and the abused (and often resentful) servant is an ancient **stereotype** (see Literary Terms) in comedy.

The comedy begins in earnest when Falstaff and his gang of thieves arrive. Notice the way it constitutes the centrepiece of the entire scene (lines 110–279), which begins with a prelude featuring trickery and ends with the introduction of the serious subject of the main plot. Falstaff's recurring complaint, that the world is full of cowards who do not keep their promises, echoes the issues of loyalty, honour and responsibility which are raised by the main **plot**. Shakespeare's **sub-plots** invariably **parody** (see Literary Terms) aspects of the main plot.

Even the thieves cannot agree what happened.

Shakespeare extracts maximum comic effect from Falstaff's capacity for lies; they grow and grow, and become so blatant that even Hal's plain speaking cannot stop them. Falstaff is, to the delight of the audience, incorrigible.

Falstaff could be leading Hal and Poins on, while sharing the joke with the audience.

The mock interview demonstrates two ways of looking at Falstaff, one bad and one good, and these perspectives are expressed in language that is highly literary and **rhetorical** (see Literary Terms). Falstaff begins by parodying a style of verse – 'King Cambyses' vein' – which was common in the Elizabethan theatre (lines 382–9). Notice the characteristics of his speech when he turns to **prose**, the **similes**, repetitions, **rhetorical questions**, verbal **antitheses** and **alliterations** (see Literary Terms). These produce an exaggerated, pompous effect suitable for his **parody** role as the king.

Falstaff's reference to 'a dagger of lath' (line 134) identifies him with the figure of Vice in the old **morality plays** (see Literary Terms), whose function was to tempt young men to sin. Prince Hal's depiction of Falstaff as 'that reverend vice, that grey iniquity, that father ruffian, that vanity in years' (lines 447–9) alludes to the character's antecedents in **morality plays**. Essentially, Hal is mocking the old man's inability to 'grow up'.

In Falstaff's speech (lines 460–74) the mood changes from comedy to something approaching **pathos** (see Literary Terms), although some actors emphasise Falstaff's capacity for self-approval here. The tone is both wheedling and touching, for Falstaff must surely realise that Hal will eventually reject him. The prince's

A glimpse of the future.   cold and terse reply, 'I do, I will' (line 475), confirms this.

GLOSSARY

7   **drawers** barmen

12   **Corinthian** 'good chap'

24   **under-skinker** under-waiter

27   **bastard** sweet Spanish wine

37   **Pomgarnet** a room in the tavern

69   **not-pated** short hair

105   **drench** medicine

117   **Titan** the sun

167   ***ecce signum*** 'behold the sign', a popular Elizabethan saying

217   **Kendal green** cloth worn by foresters and country people

232   **strappado** form of torture in which the victim was tied up by the arms, lifted, then dropped suddenly, thus jerking the arms from the sockets

266   **Hercules** Roman mythical hero famed for his feats of strength

332   **Amamon** a demon

535   **advantage** interest

538–9   **charge of foot** command of infantry

A Identify the speaker.

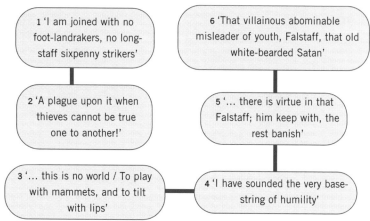

1 'I am joined with no foot-landrakers, no long-staff sixpenny strikers'

6 'That villainous abominable misleader of youth, Falstaff, that old white-bearded Satan'

2 'A plague upon it when thieves cannot be true one to another!'

5 '... there is virtue in that Falstaff; him keep with, the rest banish'

3 '... this is no world / To play with mammets, and to tilt with lips'

4 'I have sounded the very base-string of humility'

Identify the person 'to whom' this comment refers.

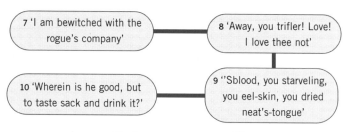

7 'I am bewitched with the rogue's company'

8 'Away, you trifler! Love! I love thee not'

10 'Wherein is he good, but to taste sack and drink it?'

9 ''Sblood, you starveling, you eel-skin, you dried neat's-tongue'

Check your answers on page 85.

B Consider these issues.

a The way Shakespeare creates atmosphere in the tavern scenes.

b The contrast between Hotspur and Hal.

c Why the Falstaffian sub-plot takes up most of the act.

d The way Shakespeare allows us to see Hotspur's domestic situation, and why.

e The effect Prince Hal creates in Scene 4.

f The way Falstaff is presented.

ACT III

SCENE 1

The division of the country would be seen as potentially disastrous by the Elizabethan audience.

Hotspur's attitude hints at divisions within the confederacy.

At the archdeacon's house in Bangor the rebels are discussing their plans. They are in an optimistic mood and certain of the support they have been promised. Owen Glendower boasts of his supernatural powers and his recent military successes against the king. Hotspur is not impressed by the self-important Welshman and mocks him. Eventually, a map is produced and the three leaders of the rebellion discuss a proposal to divide England and Wales into three regions to be ruled by Glendower, Mortimer and Harry Percy respectively. The latter objects that his share of territory is smaller than that of the other two, but after some argument concedes to the arrangement. When Glendower goes to fetch the ladies, Mortimer and Worcester take Hotspur to task for his disrespectful attitude.

Glendower returns with his Welsh-speaking daughter (Mortimer's wife) and Kate, Lady Percy. The couples bid farewell and some music is played.

COMMENT

Glendower's and Hotspur's use of language reflects their characters.

Mortimer and Glendower appear for the first time in the play. The audience has been prepared for the latter by several references to him in earlier scenes: in Act I, Scene 1 he is described as 'irregular and wild' (line 40) and in Act II, Scene 4 Falstaff says he is in league with the devil (lines 332–5). This is his only appearance, and rather than being an awe-inspiring figure, he comes across as boastful and absurdly superstitious. It should be noted that he eventually fails to join the rebel force at Shrewsbury.

Compare the characters of Glendower and Hotspur in this scene. Although we can sympathise with Hotspur's dislike of Glendower's boasting, the Welsh leader has qualities which the other cannot claim. He puts up with

Hotspur's rudeness (lines 32–4), and has a wider range of education and accomplishments. Hotspur's contempt for 'mincing poetry' (line 128), music, arcane knowledge and his 'defect of manners' (line 178) are in keeping with his 'man of action' image, but they imply limitations in his character. **Ironically** (see Literary Terms), Hotspur can be as 'wordy' as Glendower as Act I, Scene 3 shows.

Like Prince Hal in the previous scene, Hotspur is presented as a character who likes to satirise others. Their humour has a childlike quality and reflects their immaturity, since in the play they are both supposed to be young men of about the same age.

Once more, we are shown Hotspur and his wife in a moment of teasing intimacy. They only have a short time together before Hotspur goes off to fight and this final glimpse of his domestic situation adds depth to his characterisation.

GLOSSARY

13	**cressets**	lights
28	**enlargement**	freedom
31	**distemp'rature**	disorder
33	**these crossings**	oppositions
92	**moiety**	share (literally 'half')
143	**moldwarp**	mole
148	**skimble-skamble**	rumbling
171	**wilful-blam**	blameable for self-will
230	**brach**	bitch
245	**sarcenet**	thin
250	**velvet-guards**	velvet trimmings

SCENE 2

At his palace in London the king interviews the Prince of Wales. He wonders if God is punishing him for his former 'mistreadings' by giving him such a dissolute son. Prince Hal hopes to be pardoned for some of his genuine faults, but says he will refute those which are the inventions of the king's malicious flatterers. The king hopes that God at least will pardon him and then explains how he himself obtained the throne: by keeping away from common people and 'being seldom seen' (line 46) he ensured that when he did show himself he appeared all the more remarkable. Richard II, on the other hand, made himself so familiar to the populace that he lost his people's respect and was ignored.

The king compares Hal's reputation to that of Richard's, and his own when he arrived from exile, to the present standing of Hotspur whom he claims has more right to rule the country than Hal because of his many 'high deeds' (line 107) in battle. King Henry reminds his son of the present crisis, of the forces which are gathered against the throne, and fears that his own son is likely to join Percy and fight against him.

The seriousness of the meeting makes a strong contrast to the comedy of the mock interview in the tavern.

The prince solemnly promises to redeem his lost reputation by conquering Percy and asserts that he would rather die than 'break the smallest parcel of this vow' (line 159). The king promises to trust his son with an important command of his army and the scene ends with Sir Walter Blunt bringing news of the meeting of Douglas and the English rebels at

Shrewsbury. The king outlines his plans to gather his forces at Bridgnorth.

COMMENT   Once again the audience is reminded of King Henry's past (lines 4–11), his 'mistreadings' when he usurped the throne from Richard II. If Henry Bolingbroke offended God when he took the throne from Richard, then he should expect to be punished, since at the time it was assumed that kings were appointed by God to rule. When he himself is king, Prince Hal will make expiation for his father's 'sin', (cf *Henry V*).

However another view of kingship is implicit in Henry's account of how he became king (lines 39–59), and in his descriptions of Richard II and Hotspur (lines 60–84, 96–111) Henry depicts Richard as a weak and ineffectual ruler and himself as politically astute and, like Hotspur, a born leader with a 'worthy interest to the state'. If Hal, the natural successor to the throne, behaves like Richard, then by the logic of Henry's own usurpation of the throne Hotspur has more right to rule than Hal.

Prince Hal
formally accepts
his responsibilities
to the king and to
the state.

The unfavourable contrast which King Henry develops between Hotspur and Hal has its effect. The Prince of Wales vows to become a true son of his father and to exchange his own poor reputation for Hotspur's – 'exchange / His glorious deeds for my indignities' (lines 145–6). It was a convention of chivalry that a defeated champion relinquished all his honours to his victor (cf V.4.77–9).

GLOSSARY

6	**blood** offspring
16	**blood** family descent
25	**pickthanks** flatterers
50	**I stole all courtesy from heaven** I assumed a heavenly graciousness (as if my right to the throne came from God)
61	**bavin** quick-burning kindling wood

62   **carded**   scratched at and 'mingled'

69   **Enfeoff'd**   surrendered

112   **Mars in swathling clothes**   infant god of war

136   **favours**   features

SCENE 3

Falstaff's vow to repent parodies Hal's in the previous scene.

Falstaff sits in the Boar's Head tavern with a hangover from the previous night's drinking. He feels he is going into a decline and vows to repent while he still has the strength. Bardolph teases him about his size and Falstaff responds with a string of insults on the subject of Bardolph's red face, 'thou art the Knight of the Burning Lamp' (lines 25–6). The hostess enters and Falstaff has an argument with her about who picked his pockets while he was asleep. Just as Falstaff is threatening to cudgel Hal 'like a dog', the prince enters with Peto.

The hostess gets the prince on her side in the argument; Falstaff is unrepentant; and the scene ends with the prince informing the old knight that he has procured him a command of infantry. However, Falstaff will not leave the tavern until he has had his breakfast.

COMMENT

This scene winds up the comic **sub-plot** (see Literary Terms) which started with the Gad's Hill robbery. It is also the last scene set in the tavern. From now on, Falstaff will be absorbed into the main **plot** (see Literary Terms): the confrontation between the rebels and the king.

Hal tells Falstaff about the contents of his pockets (lines 155–63), picked by the prince at the end of Act II, Scene 4. Yet Falstaff will not be corrected, still persists in his lies, 'will not pocket up wrong', and forgives the hostess when she has done nothing wrong at all!

At the very end of the scene there is a change from **prose** (see Literary Terms) to verse which reflects the shift of mood from comedy to the serious concerns of the main plot. Hal has tasks for all the characters to perform, thus involving everyone in the national crisis. The tone is brisk and purposeful. Although Falstaff regrets leaving the only place he feels at home – the tavern.

GLOSSARY

2   **bate** abate, lose weight

4   **apple-john** an apple which could be kept a long time and which had wrinkled skin

18   **in good compass** within moderation

24   **admiral** flagship

29   **death's-head** skull

     memento mori Latin for 'remember you must die'

38   *ignis fatuus* will-o'-the wisp

44   **chandler** candle-maker

46   **salamander** a fabled creature said to live in fire

50   **Partlet** the name of a hen

67   **Dowlas** strong coarse linen

69   **holland** linen material

70   **ell** a measure of 45 inches (114 centimetres)

77   **denier** French coin of little value

     younker dupe

112   **Maid Marian** a lewd character from a May-game and morris-dance

156   **embossed** swollen

162   **pocket up wrong** 'swallow an insult'

Identify the speaker.

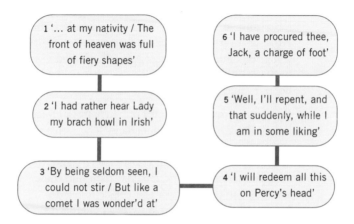

1 '... at my nativity / The front of heaven was full of fiery shapes'

6 'I have procured thee, Jack, a charge of foot'

2 'I had rather hear Lady my brach howl in Irish'

5 'Well, I'll repent, and that suddenly, while I am in some liking'

3 'By being seldom seen, I could not stir / But like a comet I was wonder'd at'

4 'I will redeem all this on Percy's head'

Identify the person 'to whom' this comment refers.

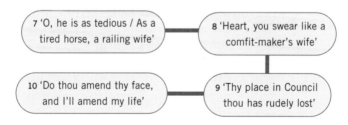

7 'O, he is as tedious / As a tired horse, a railing wife'

8 'Heart, you swear like a comfit-maker's wife'

10 'Do thou amend thy face, and I'll amend my life'

9 'Thy place in Council thou has rudely lost'

Check your answers on page 85.

 Consider these issues.

a Hotspur's behaviour at the rebels' conference.

b The way the king presents his arguments in Scene 2.

c The characterisation of women in Scenes 1 and 3.

d The developed parallel between Hotspur and Hal.

e The character of Falstaff in Scene 3.

ACT IV

SCENE 1 Hotspur, Worcester and the Earl of Douglas are in the rebel camp at Shrewsbury making preparations for war. Hotspur is pleased to have his former enemy fighting alongside him, and Douglas is equally pleased to join forces with Hotspur, whom he describes as 'the king of honour' (line 10).

This scene demonstrates the rebels' increasing isolation.

Bad news arrives in the form of letters from Hotspur's father, the Earl of Northumberland. The earl is sick and cannot come to join them in the battle. This is a serious blow, and Hotspur is at first angry and disappointed; but he and Douglas soon find some advantage in this set-back and decide to regard Northumberland's absent army as a potential reinforcement. Worcester, on the other hand, believes the absence of Northumberland will make people question the worth of the rebels' cause.

More bad news comes when Sir Richard Vernon enters with information on the advance of the king's large army. Sir Richard provides a vivid picture of the Prince of Wales in his armour, mounting his horse 'like feather'd Mercury' (line 106). Hotspur cannot wait to fight him.

The rebels learn one final piece of bad news from Vernon when he informs them that Glendower, too, will not arrive in time to fight the king. Douglas and Worcester express dismay at this, but Hotspur urges them to fight even without the help of his father and Glendower.

COMMENT Northumberland's reasons for not sending a force are unconvincing, and Worcester himself probably believes that what he says others will think: that Northumberland is afraid (lines 73–5).

The image of Prince Hal given by Vernon (lines 104–10) presents a striking contrast to the Hal we have seen previously. It is an idealised vignette of a god-like leader and occurs in a passage which is rich in chivalric **imagery** (see Literary Terms). Vernon is speaking 'outside' his character to inform the audience that Hal has reformed and is behaving like a true Prince of Wales.

Hotspur's speech in reply to Vernon (lines 111–23), contains many images associated with bloody, physical combat, which contrasts to the buoyancy of the description of Hal. But after the final piece of news, the mood of the rebels becomes fatalistic. Both they and the audience must realise that their cause is doomed to failure.

GLOSSARY

7	**soothers**	flatterers
25	**state of time**	condition of affairs
36	**advertisement**	advice
47	**main**	hand of cards
69	**off'ring**	attack
96	**daft**	tossed aside
98	**estridges**	goshawks
99	**Bated**	ruffled plumage
104	**beaver**	helmet
105	**cushes**	thigh armour
106	**Mercury**	winged messenger of Roman gods
109	**Pegasus**	winged horse of Greek myth
114	**maid of smoky war**	goddess of war
118	**reprisal**	prize

SCENE 2

Sir John Falstaff is leading his foot soldiers to Bridgnorth. He pauses to entertain the audience with an account of his conscription methods. He has misused the king's commission to conscript any man he chooses by selecting only those who are rich enough to bribe him not to take them to war. Consequently he has made over £300 and his infantry is composed of impoverished misfits. They are so badly dressed that he is ashamed to be seen with them.

Prince Hal and the Earl of Westmoreland enter and wonder if these 'pitiful rascals' are suitable soldiers, but Sir John assures them that his men are good enough to toss, that is, good enough to die in a war.

COMMENT We learn about Falstaff's 'charge of foot' and how he has come by them. His vivid account of 'pressing' functions as both satire (since this was a common practice in the 1590s) and a reflection of the less appealing aspects of his character. If Falstaff were not a comic character his indifference to his men would be repellent (lines 65–7), but the audience has been conditioned not to take him too seriously.

GLOSSARY

6 **angel** a coin worth about 50p now, but very considerably more in Shakespeare's time; so-called because the archangel Michael was stamped on it

14 **press** conscript

17 **commodity** collection

19 **caliver** small musket

20 **toasts-and-butter** well-fed

23 **ancients** ensigns

24 **gentlemen of companies** volunteers with no rank

25 **Lazarus** see Luke, 16:19–21

27 **discarded** 'sacked'

28 **revolted** runaway

29 **trade-fallen** unemployed

35 **draff** refuse

41 **gyves** fetters

66 **pit** grave

73 **three fingers** thickness of fat around Falstaff's ribs

SCENE 3 On the eve of the battle the rebels are discussing the best time to launch their attack. Hotspur wants to start

*Once again there
is disagreement
among the rebels,
which makes them
look a weakened
force.*

fighting immediately, but Worcester and Vernon advise against this because their horses are tired from the long journey to Shrewsbury. They are interrupted by the arrival of Sir Walter Blunt, who comes from the king with an offer of peace. Henry's terms are generous and include a pardon for all those involved in the rebellion. Hotspur replies by reminding Blunt (and the audience) of the rebels' grievances against the king, but he does not immediately reject the offer of peace. He tells Blunt he will send his uncle, the Earl of Worcester, with a reply in the morning.

COMMENT

*Shakespeare makes
it plain that
Henry is at fault,
but does not allow
the audience
unqualified
sympathy for the
rebels.*

Hotspur's response to Blunt is measured and satirical (lines 52–105). He reiterates the grievances he expressed in Act I, Scene 3, but in a much more detailed and methodical way. The purpose is to give the audience a full understanding of the historical background to the rebellion. Hotspur's basic points are:
- The Percy family helped Henry Bolingbroke to the throne by taking him up when he returned to England from exile
- Bolingbroke swore he only wanted his rightful title, Duke of Lancaster, returned to him
- Northumberland's good name attracted support for Bolingbroke

- Bolingbroke became ambitious and when King Richard was engaged in the Irish war he deposed him and then had him killed

- Since he has been king, Henry has behaved dishonourably, allowed Richard's heir to be held, un-ransomed, by the Welsh, broken all his original oaths, and rejected his former friends, the Percys.

It is a point in Hotspur's favour that he does not wish his list of grievances to constitute his reply to the king. He is prepared to consider Henry's offer and is quite moderate in his final words to Sir Walter Blunt: 'And may be so we shall' (line 113). Like Prince Hal, Hotspur matures during the course of the play.

GLOSSARY

26 **journey-bated** worn out from travelling

62 **sue his livery** claim his rightful dukedom

88 **personal** personally taking part

92 **in the neck of** immediately afterwards
    task'd taxed

108 **impawned** pledged

SCENE 4   The Archbishop of York supports the rebellion and he is seen sending letters to other sympathisers urging them to continue their opposition to King Henry if he wins the battle at Shrewsbury.

COMMENT   This scene takes place on the eve of the battle, at the same time as the previous one, and serves to give a heightened sense of the hopelessness of Hotspur's cause.

GLOSSARY

1 **brief** letter

10 **bide the touch** put to the test

18 **o'er-ruled by prophecies** this is another reason for Glendower's absence

31 **mo** more

A Identify the speaker.

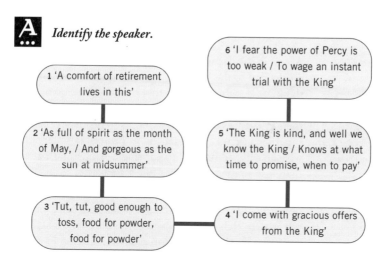

1 'A comfort of retirement lives in this'

2 'As full of spirit as the month of May, / And gorgeous as the sun at midsummer'

3 'Tut, tut, good enough to toss, food for powder, food for powder'

4 'I come with gracious offers from the King'

5 'The King is kind, and well we know the King / Knows at what time to promise, when to pay'

6 'I fear the power of Percy is too weak / To wage an instant trial with the King'

Identify the person 'to whom' this comment refers.

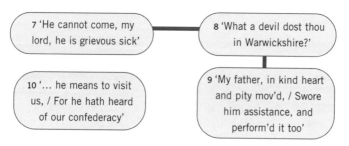

7 'He cannot come, my lord, he is grievous sick'

8 'What a devil dost thou in Warwickshire?'

9 'My father, in kind heart and pity mov'd, / Swore him assistance, and perform'd it too'

10 '... he means to visit us, / For he hath heard of our confederacy'

Check your answers on page 85.

B Consider these issues.

a How Shakespeare presents the rebels throughout this act.

b How the audience's 'sympathy' is manipulated in relation to the king and Hotspur.

c The character of Falstaff in Scene 2 and how the audience is supposed to respond to his account of conscription methods.

d The dramatic purpose of Hotspur's long speeches in Scene 3.

e The way Prince Hal and Hotspur are presented.

ACT V

SCENE 1

Once again, and for the final time, the audience is reminded of King Henry's indirect path to the throne.

An ominous dawn greets King Henry and Prince Hal on the day of the battle. A storm is approaching and the king sees this as a sign that the rebels are going to lose. Worcester and Vernon arrive and the rebels restate their grievances against the king, who dismisses them as superficial excuses for a rebellion. Prince Hal intervenes with an offer to fight Hotspur single-handed rather than lose so many lives in a full-scale battle.

The king does not agree to this and repeats his offer of peace and pardon; if Hotspur rejects the offer, he warns that 'Rebuke and dread correction' (line 111) await the rebels. When Worcester and Vernon have left, it becomes clear that neither the king nor Prince Hal believe that the rebels will accept. The scene ends with Falstaff reflecting on the nature of 'honour'.

COMMENT

Prince Hal's challenge demonstrates the sincerity of the vow he made to his father in Act III, Scene 2.

Prince Hal's willingness to fight Hotspur alone is in keeping with the chivalrous image of him in Act IV, Scene 1. He is generous in his praise of Hotspur's bravery, modest in reference to himself, 'I have a truant been to chivalry' (line 94), and shows compassionate responsibility by wanting to 'save the blood on either side' (line 99). Equally, King Henry is shown at his best in this scene, urging acceptance of his unqualified offer of peace – an offer based on consideration for all the rebel force as subjects of the king, 'We love our people well, even those we love / That are misled' (lines 104–5).

'Honour' is a recurring theme in the play, with Hotspur, that 'king of honour', as the concept's most passionate advocate. Therefore Falstaff's prosaic reflections on the subject comes at an appropriate moment in the play, just before the high ideals embodied in the word will be put to the test in a bloody conflict. Sir John's language contrasts with the exaggerated **rhetoric** (see Literary Terms) of Hotspur (see Act I, Scene 3). The older man interrogates the word's meanings from the point of view of someone who is deeply and cynically realistic. Honour is merely a word, and it leads to death.

GLOSSARY

3   **distemp'rature** cosmic disorder

17   **obedient orb** the Elizabethans believed that the planets circled the earth

19   **exhal'd** a meteor does not orbit the earth 'obediently', but has an irregular motion

29   **chewet** 'chatter-box'

40   **outdare** defy

76   **changelings** turncoats

77   **rub the elbow** show pleasure in a crowd

80   **water-colours** superficially attractive

88   **set off his head** not counted against him

130   **prick me off** kill me

139   **detraction will not suffer it** slander will not allow it to thrive

141   **scutcheon** cheap form of armorial decoration, a shield hung at funerals

SCENE 2

Falstaff's definition of honour is confirmed by Worcester's treachery.

Worcester and Vernon return to the rebel camp. Before they meet Hotspur, Worcester explains to Vernon why they should not tell him of the king's offer of peace. The earl does not trust Henry and believes that if the rebels accepted a peaceful settlement, both he and Northumberland would one day have to pay for their act of treason. Hotspur's fault would be forgiven and passed off as the product of his youthful passions, but Worcester and Northumberland would be seen as the instigators of rebellion and distrusted until they were dead. Vernon agrees to support Worcester in whatever he chooses to say.

When Hotspur appears with Douglas, Worcester tells him that the king wants to do battle. Hotspur immediately returns a defiant reply to the king. When Hotspur hears of the chivalrous challenge made by the Prince of Wales, he promises to kill him before the day is over, 'That he shall shrink under my courtesy' (line 74). After speaking some encouraging words to his troops, Hotspur leads the rebels to battle with the king.

COMMENT

Vernon speaks admiringly of Prince Hal's manner in challenging Hotspur to single combat. This annoys Hotspur and makes him even more eager to kill him, thus anticipating their inevitable confrontation.

Worcester's lie is the one serious act of treachery in the whole play. As a result, the audience's sympathy turns away from the rebels, although some remains for Hotspur, who now appears as an isolated and doomed leader.

GLOSSARY

13	**misquote**	misread
19	**spleen**	impulse
50	**tasking**	challenging
52	**urg'd**	proposed
61	**cital**	recital
66	**envy**	ill-will
91	**I profess not talking**	I don't claim to be a speaker

SCENE 3

The scene serves to illustrate the wider confusion and urgency of the battle.

In a corner of the battlefield Douglas encounters Blunt dressed as the king. He kills him and tells Hotspur that he has killed the king, but Hotspur replies that the dead man is the 'gallant knight', Sir Walter Blunt. Douglas vows to kill all those who are disguised as Henry until he meets the real king.

Falstaff enters and informs the audience that he has led nearly all the men in his command to their deaths. Prince Hal demands Falstaff's sword and when Sir John offers his 'pistol' he finds to his disgust that it is only a bottle of wine. As he leaves, Falstaff comments that he does not like the look of the kind of 'grinning honour' that led Sir Walter Blunt to his death.

COMMENT   The honourable actions of Sir Walter Blunt are contrasted to the dishonourable practice of Falstaff. It was common for unscrupulous captains to lead their men to their deaths while protecting their own lives, and then continuing to draw their soldiers' pay. Still, Falstaff's final remarks force us to reflect on the value of self-sacrificing ideals of honour.

GLOSSARY
- *21*   **furnish'd** equipped
- *25*   **coats** uniform
- *30*   **shot-free** scot-free
- *31*   **scoring** a pun on a tavern bill
- *46*   **Turk Gregory** a name synonymous with cruelty
- *68*   **carbonado** scored and grilled meat

SCENE 4

King Henry and his two sons, Prince Hal and Lord John of Lancaster, have been fighting hard and Hal has been wounded. Henry is concerned about his son and wants him to withdraw from the battle, but Hal will not leave the field while 'rebels' arms triumph in massacres!' (line 13). The two princes leave and the king is left alone. Douglas enters and attacks him. Prince Hal returns and saves his father's life. Douglas flees. King Henry acknowledges that Hal is a true and loyal son.

Prince Hal's reformation is made clear by his brave and noble actions.

The moment finally arrives when Hotspur and Prince Hal confront one another in a fight. As they are fighting Falstaff appears and cheers Hal on. He is attacked by Douglas, who leaves when Falstaff falls down as if dead.

Prince Hal fatally wounds Hotspur, who mourns the loss of his 'proud titles' (line 78) as he is dying. After speaking a generous tribute to the dead Hotspur, Hal

notices Falstaff lying on the ground. Believing he is
dead, he bids farewell to his 'old acquaintance' and
leaves.

*Falstaff's
dishonourable
conduct
counterpoints the
chivalry of
Hotspur and Hal.*

Falstaff gets up. He has been pretending to be dead and
congratulates himself on his 'discretion' in saving his
life. When he sees the dead Hotspur he stabs him to
make sure he really is dead, and then resolves to claim
that it was he who killed him.

Hal returns with his brother, and is surprised to find
Falstaff alive. Falstaff tells him that both he and
Hotspur had only been winded in the fighting. They
both rose 'at an instant, and fought a long hour by
Shrewsbury clock' (lines 146–7) until Falstaff killed
Hotspur.

Hal is amused to hear Falstaff's lie and promises to go
along with the story. A trumpet signals the defeat of
the rebels. Hal and his brother leave to inspect the
battlefield. Falstaff follows behind, the body of Hotspur
on his back, and looks forward to a reward for his
'heroism'.

COMMENT   Prince Hal demonstrates his worth as a responsible,
noble and brave heir to the throne in a sequence of
actions designed to leave the audience in no doubt

that he has honoured the vow he made to his father in
Act III, Scene 2.

- In spite of his wounds, he continues to fight
- He gives generous praise to his younger brother who
  took his place on the council (cf Act III, Scene 2)
- He saves the life of his father, thus disproving those
  who had accused him of treacherous intentions
- He fights and kills Hotspur, and pays his foe a
  magnanimous tribute
- He shows that he does not need public acclaim for
  killing Hotspur, by allowing Falstaff to take the
  credit

Note the way Shakespeare makes sure the audience
sees there has been a complete reconciliation between
King Henry and Prince Hal (lines 46–56). Hal's words
(lines 50–6) are spoken outside his character in the way
they 'interpret' his rescue of his father for the audience's
understanding.

*According to
contemporary
astrology, two
stars could not
exist in the same
sphere (cf line 64).*

When Hotspur and Hal meet, their dialogue (lines
58–69) emphasises the crucial issue which is at stake,
that England could not endure the existence of both of
them, so one must die. Notice how the way they refer
to themselves signifies both a sense of equality (both are
called Harry, both are chivalrous and brave), and an
assertion of difference (Hal's reference to himself as the
Prince of Wales and Hotspur's boast about his 'name
in arms').

*It was believed
that dying men
could foretell
the future
(cf line 82 ff).*

While Hotspur is dying it pains him most to think of
the 'proud titles' which, by the conventions of chivalry,
Hal takes from him as his victor. Yet a sense of
honourable continuity between the two is implied in
the way Hal completes Hotspur's last sentence and
moves seamlessly into his stirring tribute: 'Fare thee
well, great heart!' (line 86). Hal wishes the better part
of Hotspur, his much-praised bravery as a knight, to

live on in heaven, while his shame as a rebel dies with
him.

Hal's 'farewell'   After the prince's farewell to Falstaff comedy returns to
to Falstaff   the scene as Falstaff rises from his sham death, in
(lines 101–9) is   marked contrast with the real death of Hotspur. Once
full of puns which   again the comic mode has a critical edge which compels
refer to hunting.   the audience to reflect on the themes of the main plot.
Like his views on 'honour' (Act V, Scene 1), Falstaff's
interpretation of 'valour' is cynical and self-interested.
As he carries off the body of Hotspur, his 'trophy', his
thoughts are all on rewards and respectability.

GLOSSARY

5	**amaze**	alarm
23	**mettle**	spirit
24	**Hydra's head**	many-headed mythical monster which grew two heads for each one cut off
29	**shadows**	imitations
33	**assay**	try
65	**brook**	endure
89	**bound**	boundary
95	**favours**	the plumes from Hal's helmet
108	**Embowelled**	disembowelled (for embalming)
112–13	**termagant**	a loud unruly character
138	**Jack**	knave
159	**highest**	highest part of the battlefield
163	**purge**	here has a double meaning: to repent and to take laxatives

SCENE 5   The play ends with King Henry pronouncing
judgement on Worcester and Vernon. They are
sentenced to death for not telling Hotspur of the peace
offer and thus causing the deaths of countless
participants in the battle. We learn that Douglas has
been captured while running away; the king allows
Prince Hal to grant him a free and unconditional
pardon. Other rebels still bear arms against the king, in
Wales and in the north. King Henry arranges for his

younger son, Lord John of Lancaster, to lead a force to York to quell the army of Northumberland and the archbishop. The king and Prince Hal will go to Wales to fight Glendower and Mortimer.

COMMENT   Worcester's treachery is duly punished and Prince Hal displays generous nobility in his forgiveness of Douglas. The moral of the rebellion is drawn – it will always 'find rebuke' (line 1) in King Henry's England.

The king's plans to crush the remaining rebels anticipates *Henry IV, Part 2*, thus leaving the audience with the sense that it has seen only part of a much longer play.

GLOSSARY

4   **turn our offers contrary** make our offers the opposite of what they were

15   **pause** defer sentence

44   **leave** cease

A *Identify the speaker.*

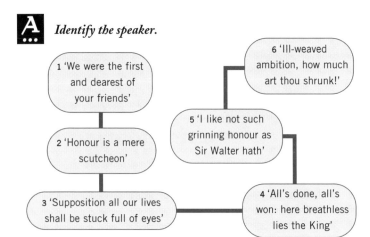

1 'We were the first and dearest of your friends'

2 'Honour is a mere scutcheon'

3 'Supposition all our lives shall be stuck full of eyes'

6 'Ill-weaved ambition, how much art thou shrunk!'

5 'I like not such grinning honour as Sir Walter hath'

4 'All's done, all's won: here breathless lies the King'

Identify the person 'to whom' this comment refers.

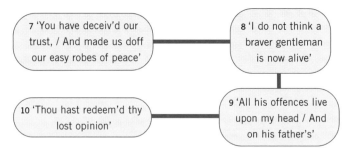

7 'You have deceiv'd our trust, / And made us doff our easy robes of peace'

8 'I do not think a braver gentleman is now alive'

10 'Thou hast redeem'd thy lost opinion'

9 'All his offences live upon my head / And on his father's'

Check your answers on page 85.

B *Consider these issues.*

a Why Worcester chooses to lie to Hotspur.

b The way Prince Hal's character is depicted throughout the scene.

c The representation of battle scenes.

d The role of Falstaff and his comic reflections on 'honour' and 'valour'.

e How the rebels are depicted before, during and after the battle.

f The effect Hotspur is supposed to have on the audience.

Part three

Commentary

Themes

Honour

'By heaven, methinks it were an easy leap / To pluck bright honour from the pale-fac'd moon' (I.3.199–200).

Hotspur's view of honour

Hotspur talks a lot about honour, and the pursuit of honour and what it means is to be an important theme in the play. To Hotspur, honour means the 'titles' won in a battle by a knight of chivalry. His imagination is fired by the 'great exploit' he anticipates, the 'blows and groans' of war, and he even talks in his sleep, according to his wife, about 'all the currents of a heady fight'. By the rules of chivalry, when he is killed all his titles of honour pass to his victor, Prince Hal; for Hotspur, this is a worse prospect than death. Hotspur's concept of honour is therefore based on physical courage and skill in battle.

Prince Hal and honour

Prince Hal talks little of honour, but his career in the play illustrates what it might mean to be an honourable leader in difficult times. At first he is an irresponsible boy who is idling away his time 'playing holidays'; his manhood has yet to be tested, and he is well aware of this. For Hal, honour becomes an issue of public responsibility, loyalty to his father's crown and the rejection of his dissolute past. The interview scene in which he promises to kill Hotspur and take away his honours for himself, 'I shall make this northern youth exchange / His glorious deeds for my indignities' (III.2.145–6), marks a significant turning point in the play, and after this reformation Hal proves true to his word. He acts decisively and calmly, winning honour in the battle and modestly letting Falstaff take the credit for Hotspur's death. In addition, Hal treats his enemies with generosity, something Hotspur does not do.

Alternative views Another perspective on honour is provided by Falstaff. He sees the wide difference between fine-sounding words like honour and what happens in the real world of combat, where these words are acted on and men meet an ugly death. 'Rare words! Brave World!' he comments, after Hal has returned from the king and is summoning them all to battle (III.3.204). Later, his catechism on honour is compelling in its bleak logic; honour is a useless word that leads to death, 'a mere scutcheon'. Immediately after this speech the audience is shown the one explicitly dishonourable act in the whole play, when Worcester decides not to tell Hotspur about the offer of peace. Worcester feels his cause as a rebel is just and honourable, but this does not stop him behaving dishonourably; he cannot believe in the devious Henry's promise of a full pardon, and so, dishonour breeds dishonour. As if to prove Falstaff's point about honour leading to death, in the next scene the honourable Sir Walter Blunt is killed while protecting the king. When Falstaff views the mangled corpse, he says, 'I like not such grinning honour as Sir Walter hath. Give me life, which if I can save, so; if not, honour comes unlooked for, and there's an end' (V.3.58–61).

POWER

Shakespeare was very interested in power. He was fascinated by the ways in which men achieve it, and how they hold on to it. Most of all, he seems to have been intrigued by the way a king can assume the role of a 'little God' and rule over other men while still being nothing more than a fallible man himself. In one of his later plays, *The Tragedy of King Lear*, he depicts a king stripped of his power and realising it has been a fraud:

'They told me I was everything; 'tis a lie, I am not ague-proof.'

When he was Henry Bolingbroke, King Henry had challenged the assumption that the king had a divine right to rule, that he was 'God's substitute' on earth. He saw Richard II as a weak and incompetent ruler. Through a combination of force and political skill, he snatched the throne from Richard and made himself king. At the start of *Henry IV, Part 1*, the king's problem is how to legitimise his assumption of authority in a country that is beleaguered by strife. Resistance to Henry's rule is coming from Scotland and Wales, from the powerful Percy family in the north, from the church, and perhaps even from his own son, who is irresponsible and cannot be trusted to take his place on the governing council. In addition, Henry's conscience troubles him for his past 'mistreadings'. He dreams of finding atonement and unifying his country under the banner of a crusade to the Holy Land, where all the opposing forces will 'in mutual well-beseeming ranks, / March all one way' (I.1.14–15).

Henry needs to justify his authority.

Henry deals with these problems efficiently. He makes Hal reform and fights the rebels. Unlike King Richard, he knows how important it is to win support by calculating the effect he has on his people. So, by all practical standards, he is a good king. But Henry is still a king who has sinned against God, therefore if he is to legitimise his usurping of the throne he must demonstrate that his successor, Prince Hal, would make a worthy ruler. Henry knows that as a usurper he is vulnerable to others claiming the throne; through Hal he can perhaps re-establish the right of linear descent.

Prince Hal shows that he is fit to be king in a number of ways. Like his father he can 'perform' the political and theatrical roles to manipulate people or fight off rivals like Hotspur. Also like his father he is calculating

THEMES continued

Prince Hal will make a good king.

enough to cast off his friends when they cease to be of use to him. Hal, however, shows he has more humanity than his father. He seems to have a genuine affinity with his low-life companions. And in the qualities of generosity, modesty and mercy, he shows he is more chivalrous than Hotspur, the character who haunts Henry because he reminds him of himself when he started his illegitimate journey to the throne (see III.2.93–6).

STRUCTURE

The events in the play take place in several different locations. This is because Shakespeare was trying to represent the diversity in English national life and how this diversity might threaten the unified state which Henry wants to create. The scenes move from the king's palace in London and the Council Chamber at Windsor Castle to places as far removed as Warkworth Castle and York in the north and Bangor in Wales, interspersed with socially obscure locations such as the inn yard in Rochester, the highway at Gad's Hill, the Boar's Head tavern in Eastcheap and a road near Coventry. The final act is set in different parts of the field of battle at Shrewsbury. Some of the scenes follow one another to create the illusion of things taking place at the same time, such as the second scene in Act I where Hal is shown talking to Falstaff; others occur chronologically, like the final scene of the same act in which the rebels have come to Windsor to meet the king as he commanded in Scene 1, on 'Wednesday next'.

The different locations reflect a variety of views.

A useful way to approach the structure of the play is to think of the different groups of characters who are associated with these diverse scenes. First there is King

Henry and his court who are only shown in the chambers of power in London and Windsor, and on the battlefield at Shrewsbury. This emphasises a certain regal distance between the king and his country. The rebels and their sympathisers appear in several locations: at court, at the Percy family's castle in Northumberland, at the archdeacon's house in Bangor and the archbishop's palace in York. This reinforces the sense of a fractured state, with discontent and threat coming from places as far apart as Wales and the north of England. Then there is the group of characters who make up the **sub-plot** (see Literary Terms). The main focus for these is the Boar's Head tavern in Eastcheap where the great comic scenes are played. This group of tapsters, carriers, rich travellers, robbers and con-artists reflect something of the unmanageable diversity of English social life. As the main **plot** (see Literary Terms) and the **sub-plot** merge, only Prince Hal and Falstaff show the connections between these localised elements.

The two plots

Shakespeare deploys the standard five-act form of Elizabethan drama which allows him to develop, scene by scene, alternating aspects of the main plot and the sub-plot. The relationship between the two plots is reflective, with the comic sub-plot often parodying the subject of the main plot. Thus in Act I two conspiracies are begun, the rebels' conspiracy against the king, which will be the subject of the main plot, and the comic sub-plot conspiracy against Falstaff. Within this form, contrast becomes a basic dramatic principle, not only the contrast between the main plot and sub-plot, but between individual characters and groups of characters.

The play is full of contrasts.

For example, Hal and Hotspur are contrasted as types of potential ruler; King Henry and Falstaff are contrasted as father figures; and Hotspur's devotion to the ideals of chivalry is contrasted with Falstaff's determination to survive the battle with or without honour.

As is customary in Shakespeare's plays, the climax of the comic **sub-plot** occurs before the climax of the main **plot**. After Falstaff's lies have been unmasked, the comedy turns to the specific subject of the main plot, namely the impending interview between Hal and the king. From there on Falstaff's role is to provide satirical reflections on the action of the main plot, right up to the slaying of Hotspur by Hal.

At the end of the play, some kind of resolution is achieved when the king passes judgement on his enemies, but his problems are far from over. His last words anticipate future problems and another play.

CHARACTERS

KING HENRY IV

When he was Henry Bolingbroke, cousin of King Richard II, Henry returned to England from exile and received help from the Percy family in reclaiming his title and lands, the duchy of Lancaster. He later usurped the throne from Richard and rejected the Percys. At the start of the play, Henry is a king with much on his mind: his indirect path to the throne, combined with his treatment of his former supporters, has caused dissension and civil unrest; he is afraid that his son, the irresponsible Prince of Wales, is not a fit person to inherit the throne; and he desperately wants to unify the country under his rule and suppress Mortimer, Earl of March, another of Richard's cousins who has a better claim to the throne than himself.

Guilty
Shrewd
Calculating
Controlled
Self-righteous

Henry IV is not a very attractive character. Formal and strained in speech, he comes across as guarded and deceitful in the opening scenes of the play. He is defensive when Worcester reminds him of his debt to the Percys (I.3) and angrily denies that Mortimer ever fought with Glendower (I.3). All this indicates a man who is troubled by his conscience and fearful for his position as King of England. At first the audience is likely to sympathise with the rebels against 'this ingrate and canker'd Bolingbroke', 'this king of smiles', because it has learnt from them about his past and heard how badly he has treated the Percys.

King Henry, however, is a deeply politicised figure in the play and his function is to focus the audience's attention on the issue of power and the line of rightful authority. He knows he may have sinned against God for his past 'mistreadings', and the prospect of his eldest son, the heir to the throne, failing to meet his responsibilities, fills him with dread. It was these same weaknesses in Richard II that partly justified the usurpation, and Henry fears that in the dissolute behaviour of Hal he is experiencing God's punishment.

In Act III, Scene 2 Henry describes to Hal how he won popular support while planning to take the crown from Richard (lines 39–59). He is proud of his ability to manipulate 'opinion' and presents himself as a shrewd and calculating politician, in contrast to the careless and self-indulgent Richard. As soon as he has gained from his son a promise to loyally fight the rebels, Henry reveals his total command of the practicalities of battle. He makes quick decisions. He assembles his forces at Bridgnorth and demonstrates generosity to the rebels with an offer of peace. Unlike the rebels, King Henry is concerned for the welfare of the whole state. This is something he makes plain to Worcester in Act V: 'We love our people well, even those we love / That are misled' (lines 104–5). Whether or not the rebels are right to distrust him, at the end of the play Henry makes what appears to be a genuine attempt to avoid loss of life on both sides. And after the battle has been won, he is presented as a ruler firmly in command of the situation, righteous in his 'rebuke' of Worcester and Vernon, and merciful to some of the other rebels.

PRINCE HAL

Diplomatic
Self-aware
Fun-loving
Courageous
Honourable

Hal's character changes during the course of the play and the process of this change forms an essential part of the plot. Like his father, he is capable of a diplomatic concealment of his true intentions and an awareness of the public 'effect' he has to achieve as a responsible Prince of Wales. This awareness is confided to the audience early in the play, in his only **soliloquy** (see Literary Terms): 'So, when this loose behaviour I throw off, / And pay the debt I never promised, / By how much better than my word I am, / By so much shall I falsify men's hopes' (I.2.203–6).

Hal is so aware of himself that he even intends to use his faults as a means of achieving public acclaim: 'I'll so offend, to make offence a skill' (I.2.211). Thus, from the start of the play, the audience is watching Hal as a king in the making.

We first encounter Hal in conversation with Falstaff (I.2). He is witty and energetic. He loves teasing his old friend about his drunkenness and dishonesty. He clearly has no illusions about Falstaff and participates in the robbery only far enough to make a fool of him. Hal's moral detachment makes him look calculating, but Shakespeare's dramatic purpose here is to make sure that Hal does nothing that will blemish his later image as the fully reformed Prince of Wales. Indeed, the Gad's Hill adventure and subsequent roistering in the Eastcheap tavern can be seen as the adventurous spirits of a young man of high position who communicates with all levels of society. As he says, 'I have sounded the very base-string of humility' (II.4.5–6).

Prince Hal's character changes after the interview with
his father in Act III. During this difficult encounter he
shows himself to be contrite in admitting his faults, and
sincere in his vow to accept his responsibilities and
behave more like a true son to the king: 'I shall here-
after, my thrice gracious lord, / Be more myself'
(III.2.92–3). When he realises how much his own
father distrusts him, he is deeply moved to make
amends for his lost reputation and promises to 'redeem
all this on Percy's head' (III.2.132).

After this, Hal proves he is capable of turning his words
into actions. He returns briskly to the Boar's Head, a
champion of 'faith, truth and honesty', and summons
Falstaff to fight for his King. We see him, through the
words of Vernon, mounting his war-horse 'As if an
angel dropp'd down from the clouds / To turn and
wind a fiery Pegasus' (IV.1.108–9) and we witness his
noble challenge to meet Hotspur in single combat, 'to
save the blood on either side' (V.1.99). When the battle
commences Hal fights courageously, in spite of his
wounds, and wins his father's trust by saving his life.
But the supreme confirmation of his worth comes when
he kills Hotspur. He does not gloat over the death of
his foe; he pays him a generous and honourable tribute,
and later allows Falstaff to take the credit, thus
demonstrating that for him honour resides in the act
itself and not in the reward of public acclaim.

Harry percy, hotspur

Impulsive

Brave

Tactless

Humorous

Emotional

Harry Percy, as his nickname 'Hotspur' implies, has an
impatient, excitable nature. A courageous knight, he is
famous for winning honours in battle. Honour, in fact,
is much on his mind throughout the course of the play;
when he is dying, it is the loss of honour that upsets
him more than his approaching death.

Hotspur's impulsiveness, his determined tendency to speak his mind at whatever the cost, makes him a difficult person for the other rebels to deal with. After he has met the king in Act I, his father and uncle have to restrain him from giving vent to his anger and indignation. Unlike Worcester, Hotspur is tactless and undiplomatic, and it is Worcester who provides the most telling criticism of Hotspur's character (III.1.171–83). Worcester's point is that while Hotspur's brave determination is a good quality in a knight, when it leads to outbursts of rage and indiscretion it makes people lose faith. If Hotspur cannot govern himself, how can he govern others?

However, Hotspur's devotion to battle suits the purposes of his scheming uncle well. His gift for vivid, declamatory speeches makes him a good man to lead the troops into action. And he is more than ready to set himself in implacable opposition to King Henry. Hotspur is an interesting character and during the play we learn several things about him which reflect Shakespeare's ability to create richly varied individuals:

- In spite of his claim to despise 'mincing poetry', Hotspur uses language with great imagination, as when he describes to the king the appearance and manner of the emissary after the battle of Holmedon (I.3.32–63), or his picture of Mortimer fighting on 'the gentle Severn's sedgy bank' (I.3.97). This gift often runs away with itself, usually when Hotspur is thinking of a battle in which he will win honour. As his father says, 'Imagination of some great exploit / Drives him beyond the bounds of patience' (I.3.197–8).

- Hotspur's impatience to get to war makes him forgetful and careless. He arrives at Bangor without his map, and earlier cannot remember the name of the castle in which he first met Henry Bolingbroke.

- Unlike Prince Hal, his counterpart in the play, Hotspur seems to be ruled by his emotions. His wife, Kate, gives us an interesting glimpse of what it is like to live with such a highly charged character when she describes his state of mind at home in Warkworth Castle: 'Why hast thou lost the fresh blood in thy cheeks, / And given my treasures and my rights of thee / To thick-ey'd musing, and curst melancholy?' (II.3.45–7). Later, she describes him as someone 'altogether govern'd by humours'.

- Hotspur can be very comical. He contributes some wonderful satire to the play, notably his depiction of the 'certain lord' who annoys him so much at Holmedon. And his debunking of Glendower's pretensions reveals an ability to combine logical argument with ridicule to devastating effect.

- In spite of the misfortunes which the rebels experience before the battle, Hotspur remains optimistic, though his impatient determination to fight is qualified by his willingness to reflect on the king's offer of peace. A more mature Hotspur begins to emerge towards the end. He provides the most comprehensive account of the rebels' cause (IV.3). And although he never matches Prince Hal in 'courtesy', the tribute which the prince pays him seems perfectly fitting: 'This earth that bears thee dead / Bears not alive so stout a gentleman' (V.4.91–2).

FALSTAFF
Witty
Contradictory
Gluttonous
Self-interested
Dishonourable

Falstaff is the main source of comedy in the play. He is one of the most wonderful and popular characters Shakespeare ever invented. It is said that Queen Elizabeth I liked him so much that she asked Shakespeare to write another play featuring Falstaff as a lover; this became *The Merry Wives of Windsor*.

Falstaff is based on Sir John Oldcastle, who had been highly regarded by Henry V (formerly Prince Hal) until he became a heretic and was executed in 1417. Shakespeare wanted to use the name 'Oldcastle' at first, but changed it to Falstaff after Sir John Oldcastle's descendants objected. However, there is probably nothing in the character of Falstaff which resembles Oldcastle. Shakespeare's creation is wholly original, a force of irreverent comedy with which everyone can identify. Falstaff is not so much a person, to be judged by realistic standards, as a function. Part comic fool and part vice figure from the **morality plays** (see Literary Terms), his role embodies such a rich mixture of qualities that it is impossible to characterise him in simple terms. Here are some basic points which should be kept in mind when considering his character:

- Falstaff is the play's Fool and, like all Shakespeare's Fools, he shows considerable virtuosity with language. He turns words inside out, deliberately mistakes what people say to him, moralises satirically on the serious themes of the play (such as honour), boasts and lies without shame, and is not ruled by the kind of conventions which influence 'ordinary' characters.
- Falstaff is Hal's closest friend and at times he treats the young prince with almost paternal tenderness. This feeling is reciprocated, but it is strictly qualified by Hal's awareness of Falstaff's weaknesses, his potential to 'mislead' him.
- Falstaff's speeches are often partly aimed at the audience, inviting it to collude with his hilarious dishonesty, his jokes and his excuses rather in the manner of a music-hall comedian. In performance this should be especially evident in Act II, Scene 4, where Falstaff could be played as if he were leading Hal and Poins on with his lies, that are 'gross as a mountain, open, palpable', while all the time sharing the joke with the audience.

- Dramatically Falstaff's world of idleness, dishonesty, self-indulgence and irresponsibility is in direct contrast to the honour and nobility which Prince Hal finally achieves. By integrating him so completely into the action, Shakespeare ensures that the audience is continually provided with an alternative perspective to the serious themes. Even when Falstaff is being blatantly corrupt and dishonourable, the audience cannot dislike him because it has been taught to identify with his irrepressible humour and will to live.

THE REBELS: WORCESTER, NORTHUMBERLAND, MORTIMER AND GLENDOWER

We first hear about Worcester in the opening scene of the play. He is blamed for Hotspur's refusal to surrender the prisoners. Westmoreland describes him as 'malevolent' to the king 'in all aspects'. Worcester's is the scheming mind behind the rebellion. This becomes clear when Henry confronts him at Windsor: 'I do see / Danger and disobedience in thine eye' (I.3.14–15). Later Worcester confirms Henry's instinctive fear by revealing to Hotspur the 'secret book' of his plans. Of all the rebels Worcester is the most calculating. He deeply distrusts Henry and believes that if the offer of peace is accepted, both he and Northumberland will still be killed. Because of this, he lies to Hotspur, telling him the king wants to fight.

Northumberland and Mortimer have quite small parts in the play. Neither fight in the battle at Shrewsbury, Northumberland because he is sick, and Mortimer because he is involved with Glendower's Welsh forces. Northumberland is Hotspur's father and, like his uncle, Worcester, finds the young knight's petulant behaviour inappropriate.

MORTIMER

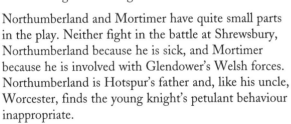

Mortimer is Hotspur's brother-in-law and has married Glendower's daughter, with whom he is besotted even though he cannot speak Welsh and she cannot speak English. Glendower also does not come to join the battle at Shrewsbury. He is a proud, learned and valiant leader, but his long-winded pretentiousness irritates Hotspur.

THE ROBBERS: POINS, PETO, BARDOLPH AND GADSHILL

Poins has been a close companion of Falstaff for many years. He is sharp and witty, a practised hoaxer, who obviously finds Hal's idea of a joke somewhat inept (II.4). It is Poins who thinks up the joke against Falstaff. Gadshill plans the robbery and goes out to Rochester ahead of the others to identify the victims. He is a professional thief and, appropriately, takes his name from a place which was famous for highway robberies, Gad's Hill in Kent. Bardolph has a more prominent part than Peto. Like Sir John, he is devoted to sack and his red face is the subject of several jokes.

THE LADIES: KATE, LADY PERCY, LADY MORTIMER AND MISTRESS QUICKLY (THE HOSTESS)

It is interesting that Shakespeare chooses to show the rebels Hotspur, Mortimer and Glendower in relation to close female relatives. Hotspur's wife, Kate, is an intelligent, assertive woman who wants to be more involved in her distracted husband's affairs, but Hotspur keeps her at a distance with his **ironic** (see Literary Terms) teasing: there is no place for a woman in his masculine world of battle and the pursuit of honour. He does, however, take her to the rebels' meeting at Bangor, and it is there that we meet Glendower's Welsh-speaking daughter who is also Mortimer's wife. She is clearly besotted with Mortimer, as he is with her, and she does not want him to go to war. These glimpses into the private lives of the rebels make them look vulnerable and, by the standards of the time, enfeebled. In Shakespeare's day women were considered irrational and not capable of the kind of reasoned, dutiful responsibilities which men had to undertake. (Note the words of Northumberland's rebuke to Hotspur, Act I, Scene 3, lines 233–34.)

Mistress Quickly is the hostess of the Boar's Head tavern in Eastcheap. She is a forthright woman and is not afraid to give Falstaff a piece of her mind, even if he is a knight.

LANGUAGE AND STYLE

Henry IV, Part 1 belongs to the middle period of Shakespeare's career, a period in which many people believe he achieved the perfect balance between thought and expression. Although the play is not especially 'poetic' in the way his later plays are, it still contains passages of vivid **imagery** (see Literary Terms). Sometimes this is designed to create a picture in the mind of the audience and effect an emotional response, as in some of Hotspur's speeches on the subject of fighting and honour; at other times the imagery is intended to express complex ideas, such as Hal's **soliloquy** (see Literary Terms) at the end of Act I, Scene 2. Throughout the play there is a wide variety of language styles which reflect different aspects of the characters and the action. The diversity of style appears in the customary forms of **blank verse** and **prose** (see Literary Terms).

Blank verse

Blank verse is used in the play for its normal purposes, that is, to heighten the importance of the ideas and emotions, and to reflect the higher status of certain groups of characters. It does not rhyme, except sometimes in the last two lines of a speech where an emphasis may be required. It has the same rhythm, or **metre**, of five **iambs** (see Literary Terms) and is close to the stresses of spoken English. It is very flexible and long sentences can be built up into **verse paragraphs** (see Literary Terms). An example worth analysing is the opening speech of the play where King Henry unfolds a long chain of **imagery** (see Literary Terms) all associated with his preoccupation with the dangers of civil conflict and disruption. Blank verse is nearly always used by characters involved in the main **plot** (see Literary Terms).

Prose

Prose (see also Literary Terms) is most often given to minor or comic characters in the play. There is a great deal of prose in *Henry IV, Part 1* because the comic **sub-plot** (see Literary Terms) takes up so much of the action.

The different styles of speech used in the play

In *Henry IV, Part 1*, Shakespeare encompasses a wide range of social and national life and this is reflected in the many different language styles and speech **registers** (see Literary Terms) that can be found in the play. There is the language of the court with its formal, convoluted sentences and the informal language of the tavern full of rich local details of Elizabethan life. Between these extremes, are numerous registers that capture both the individual situation of the characters and the interplay of thematic ideas: Hotspur's extravagant references to honour and chronicle-like speeches about Henry's past reflect his identification with the values of chivalry; Falstaff's prosaic reflections on honour reveal a cynical distrust of such idealism. Equally, Glendower's speeches contain **allusions** (see Literary Terms) to the mysteries of an ancient Welsh culture, allusions which are ridiculed in the blunt logic of Hotspur's replies. When Hal is in the tavern he is pleased to be able to speak with the humble drawers in their own 'language', thus demonstrating an affinity with the people he will one day rule. And he matches Falstaff in 'quips' and 'quiddities', though it is the latter's speech style which is not surprisingly the most memorable in the play. Falstaff's speeches are rich in Biblical and classical **allusions, parodies** of popular Elizabethan theatre, **puns**, quibbles, inventive insults, all of which express his embodiment of **wit** (see Literary Terms).

Part four

Study skills

How to use quotations

One of the secrets of success in writing essays is the way you use quotations. There are five basic principles:
- Put inverted commas at the beginning and end of the quotation
- Write the quotation exactly as it is in the original
- Do not use a quotation that repeats what you have just written
- Use the quotation so that it fits into your sentence
- Keep the quotation as short as possible

Quotations should be used to develop the line of thought in your essays.

Your comment should not duplicate what is in your quotation. For example:

> **Hotspur thinks King Henry is vile; he calls him 'this vile politician'.**

Far more effective is to write:

> **Hotspur's contempt for King Henry 's deviousness is expressed in extreme terms: 'this vile politician Bolingbroke'.**

Always lay out the lines as they appear in the text. For example:

> **King Henry uses vivid personification to express the horrors of civil war: No more the thirsty entrance to this soil**
>
> **Shall daub her lips with her own children's blood**

However, the most sophisticated way of using the writer's words is to embed them into your sentence:

> **Hotspur's promise 'to lift the down-trod Mortimer' shows his tendency for emotional over-statement.**

When you use quotations in this way, you are showing you can use text as evidence to support your ideas.

Everyone writes differently. Work through the suggestions given here and adapt the advice to suit your own style and interests. This will improve your essay-writing skills and allow your personal voice to emerge.

The following points indicate in ascending order the skills of essay writing:

- Picking out one or two facts about the story and adding the odd detail
- Writing about the text by retelling the story
- Retelling the story and adding a quotation here and there
- Organising an answer which explains what is happening in the text and giving quotations to support what you write

....

- Writing in such a way as to show that you have thought about the intentions of the writer of the text and that you understand the techniques used
- Writing at some length, giving your viewpoint on the text and commenting by picking out details to support your views
- Looking at the text as a work of art, demonstrating clear critical judgement and explaining to the reader of your essay how the enjoyment of the text is assisted by literary devices, linguistic effects and psychological insights; showing how the text relates to the time when it was written

The dotted line above represents the division between lower and higher level grades. Higher-level performance begins when you start to consider your response as a reader of the text. The highest level is reached when you offer an enthusiastic personal response and show how this piece of literature is a product of its time.

Coursework
Essay

Set aside an hour or so at the start of your work to plan what you have to do.

- List all the points you feel are needed to cover the task. Collect page references of information and quotations that will support what you have to say. A helpful tool is the highlighter pen: this saves painstaking copying and enables you to target precisely what you want to use.

- Focus on what you consider to be the main points of the essay. Try to sum up your argument in a single sentence, which could be the closing sentence of your essay. Depending on the essay title, it could be a statement about a character: Prince Hal is more chivalrous than Hotspur. He pays him several generous tributes and declines to take the credit for killing him; an opinion about setting: Shakespeare sets the play in many different locations. This gives the impression of the rich diversity of English national life; or a judgement on a theme: I believe the main theme of the play is the struggle to maintain power. By the end, Prince Hal has shown that he has the necessary qualities to be a good ruler in difficult times.

- Make a short essay plan. Use the first paragraph to introduce the argument you wish to make. In the following paragraphs develop this argument with details, examples and other possible points of view. Sum up your argument in the last paragraph. Check you have answered the question.

- Write the essay, remembering all the time the central point you are making.

- On completion, go back over what you have written to eliminate careless errors and improve expression. Read it aloud to yourself, or, if you are feeling more confident, to a relative or friend.

If you can, try to type your essay, using a word processor. This will allow you to correct and improve your writing without spoiling its appearance.

Examination
essay

The essay written in an examination often carries more marks than the coursework essay even though it is written under considerable time pressure.

In the revision period build up notes on various aspects of the text you are using. Fortunately, in acquiring this set of York Notes on *Henry IV, Part 1*, you have made a prudent beginning! York Notes are set out to give you vital information and help you to construct your personal overview of the text.

Make notes with appropriate quotations about the key issues of the set text. Go into the examination knowing your text and having a clear set of opinions about it.

In most English Literature examinations you can take in copies of your set books. This in an enormous advantage although it may lull you into a false sense of security. Beware! There is simply not enough time in an examination to read the book from scratch.

In the
examination

- Read the question paper carefully and remind yourself what you have to do.
- Look at the questions on your set texts to select the one that most interests you and mentally work out the points you wish to stress.
- Remind yourself of the time available and how you are going to use it.
- Briefly map out a short plan in note form that will keep your writing on track and illustrate the key argument you want to make.
- Then set about writing it.
- When you have finished, check through to eliminate errors.

To summarise,   • Know the text
these are the   • Have a clear understanding of and opinions on the storyline,
keys to success: characters, setting, themes and writer's concerns
   • Select the right material
   • Plan and write a clear response, continually bearing the question
   in mind

SAMPLE ESSAY PLAN

A typical essay question on *Henry IV, Part 1* is followed by a sample essay plan in note form. This does not present the only answer to the question, merely one answer. Do not be afraid to use your own ideas and leave out some of the ones in this sample! Remember that quotations are essential to support and illustrate the points you make.

What do you learn about the character of Hotspur during the course of the play?

Introduction   This should clearly outline how you are going to deal with the question. It should briefly summarise Hotspur's role in the play, the good and bad qualities, and your general view of his function.

Part 1   Here you might try to review all the details which are relevant to building up a picture of Hotspur's character:
* His reaction to the king in Act I, Scene 3. His identification with 'honour'
* His behaviour at home with his wife, Kate. His obsession with war
* Prince Hal's parody of Hotspur in Act II, Scene 4
* His rudeness to Glendower in Act III, Scene 1, and what his uncle, Worcester, says about him. His attitude to poetry and music and Kate's comment that he is 'altogether govern'd by humours'
* His response to the news of his father's sickness in Act IV, Scene 1

- His response to Vernon's description of Hal in the same scene
- The way he presents the rebels' case to Blunt in Act IV, Scene 3, and his decision to consider the offer of peace
- His behaviour on the battlefield and what he says while he is dying. The respect which Prince Hal feels for him

Part 2   In this part you should evaluate the essential points that can be learnt from Hotspur's role in the play:
- The kind of honour with which Hotspur is identified, his chivalry and eagerness to fight
- The way the faults in his character work against him as a potential leader. His lack of self-control and diplomacy
- Shakespeare's dramatic reasons for sustaining an implicit comparison between Hotspur and Prince Hal

Conclusion   This will draw all the material you have used in the main body of the essay together, but should not reiterate everything you have written. You should summarise the evidence for your own particular opinion of Hotspur, and provide key references to support your view.

FURTHER QUESTIONS

Make a plan as shown above and attempt these questions.

1 Describe how Shakespeare presents the rebels and their cause.
2 Trace the development of the sub-plot throughout the play and describe how it relates to the main plot.
3 How does Shakespeare control the audience's sympathy in the play?

4 Make a comparison between the characters of Hotspur and Prince Hal.

5 Review some of the changes to historical fact which Shakespeare made in the play and explain the dramatic reasons for this.

6 Write a detailed analysis of the role of Falstaff in the play.

7 Is Prince Hal really honourable? Write a critical analysis of his characterisation in the play.

8 Evaluate the character of Hotspur in terms of his own words and those of the people who know him best.

9 'We cannot condemn Falstaff because he is protected by his comic role in the play'. Discuss this statement.

10 Compare the roles of King Henry and Falstaff in relation to Prince Hal.

11 Describe how Shakespeare creates a sense of English national life in the play.

12 Discuss the themes of power and honour and show how they are expressed in *Henry IV, Part 1*.

PART FIVE

CULTURAL CONNECTIONS

BROADER PERSPECTIVES

Shakespeare's sources

The Prince by Machiavelli (1513). A book of political advice to rulers, widely influential in Shakespeare's day. It recommended the need sometimes to lie to the populace for their own good and to preserve power. 'Machiavel' was used to describe practised liars and political opportunists. Some critics believe the history plays reveal Machiavelli's influence on Shakespeare's understanding of political power and change.

Chronicles of England by Raphael Holinshed (2nd edition, 1587). This was the major source of Shakespeare's knowledge of history. It is a fascinating, shapeless hotchpotch of historical odds and ends, anecdotes, stories and distortions of fact by the Tudors' favourite historian.

A Myyoure for Magistrates (1559). A large collection of stories, one of which tells how Owen Glendower made himself the Prince of Wales.

On Shakespeare's history plays

Shakespeare's History Plays – Richard II to Henry V, ed. G. Holderness, Macmillan (1992). A collection of critical essays by contemporary critics who seek to challenge orthodox interpretations of Shakespeare.

Background works

The Terrible Tudors by Terry Deary and Neil Tongue, Scholastic Publications (1993). An entertaining, informative and accessible account of the period.

The Shakespearean Stage (1574–1642) by A. Gurr, Cambridge University Press (1970). A useful study of the theatres, companies, actors and stage conditions of Shakespeare's time.

Film

Chimes at Midnight, 1966, directed by Orson Welles. Drawn from Shakespeare's history plays, this superb film contains an incomparable realisation of the battle of Shrewsbury.

allusion reference which briefly recalls something in another text

alliteration sequence of repeated consonants in poetry or prose

antithesis opposing or contrasting ideas in following sentences or clauses, using opposite or contrasting forms of words

blank verse unrhymed line of five iambs

diction the choice of words in a work of literature

dramatic irony occurs when the plot develops in such a way that the audience has more information about what is happening than some of the characters themselves

genre type of literature, e.g. tragedy or comedy

hyperbole figure of speech which relies on exaggeration

iamb metrical foot, or pattern, in which a weak stress is followed by a strong stress, ti-tum

iambic pentameter a line of five iambic feet; the most common metrical pattern in English verse

imagery a word picture using a metaphor or simile

ironic/irony saying one thing while meaning something else

metaphor comparison between two different things, e.g. 'that roasted Manningtree ox ...' as a reference to Falstaff

metre the pattern of stressed and unstressed syllables in a line of verse

morality plays plays written and performed between about 1450 and 1550. They had Christian themes and often contained a character called the Vice, a half-comic, half-evil tempter

parody imitation of a specific work of literature (prose or verse) or style which deliberately ridicules its characteristic features

pathos depiction of events which evoke strong feelings of pity or sorrow

personification where things or ideas are treated as if they were human beings, with human attributes and feelings

plot the plan of a literary work

prose language that is not patterned by the regularity of some kind of metre

pun a play on words; two quite different meanings are drawn from a single word, usually for comic purposes

register the language used for a specific situation or purpose

rhetoric the art of speaking (or writing) persuasively

rhetorical questions these are asked not for the sake of enquiry, but for emphasis: the speaker expects the audience to be convinced of the reply's appropriateness

riddle deliberately puzzling way of referring to an object or an idea

simile figure of speech in which one thing is said to be like another; a simile always contains the word 'like' or 'as'

soliloquy dramatic convention which allows a character in a play to speak directly to the audience as if thinking aloud about motives, feelings and decisions

stereotype a standard, fixed idea or mental impression

sub-plot subsidiary action running parallel with the main plot of a play or novel

symbol something which represents something else by analogy or association

tragedy drama that traces the career and downfall of an individual

verse paragraphs in poetry, an extended sentence, or group of sentences, over several lines

wit originally meaning 'sense', 'understanding' or 'intelligence', the word came to refer to the kind of poetic intelligence which combines or contrasts ideas and expressions in an unexpected and intellectually pleasing way

TEST ANSWERS

TEST YOURSELF (Act I)

1 King Henry *(1.5–6)*
2 Prince Hal *(2.2)*
3 Falstaff *(2.92)*
4 Worcester *(3.10–11)*
5 Hotspur *(3.133–4)*
6 Northumberland *(3.272)*
7 Hotspur *(1.80)*
8 Falstaff *(2.180–2)*
9 Worcester *(3.14–15)*
10 Hotspur *(3.233–4)*

TEST YOURSELF (Act II)

1 Gadshill *(1.72–3)*
2 Falstaff *(2.27–8)*
3 Hotspur *(3.92–3)*
4 Hal *(4.5–6)*
5 Falstaff *(4.424–5)*
6 Hal *(4.456–7)*
7 Poins *(2.17)*
8 Kate *(3.91)*
9 Hal *(4.240–1)*
10 Falstaff *(4.449–50)*

TEST YOURSELF (Act III)

1 Glendower *(1.11–12)*
2 Hotspur *(1.230)*
3 King Henry *(2.46–7)*
4 Hal *(2.132)*

5 Falstaff *(3.4–5)*
6 Hal *(3.185)*
7 Glendower *(1.153–4)*
8 Kate *(1.241–2)*
9 Hal *(2.32)*
10 Bardolph *(3.23)*

TEST YOURSELF (Act IV)

1 Douglas *(1.56)*
2 Vernon *(1.101–2)*
3 Falstaff *(2.65–6)*
4 Blunt *(3.30)*
5 Hotspur *(3.52–3)*
6 Archbishop of York *(4.19–20)*
7 Northumberland *(1.16)*
8 Hal *(2.50–1)*
9 Northumberland *(3.64–5)*
10 King Henry *(4.37–8)*

TEST YOURSELF (Act V)

1 Worcester *(1.33)*
2 Falstaff *(1.140–1)*
3 Worcester *(2.8)*
4 Douglas *(3.16)*
5 Falstaff *(3.67–8)*
6 Hal *(4.87)*
7 Worcester *(1.11–12)*
8 Hotspur *(1.89–91)*
9 Hotspur *(2.20–1)*
10 Hal *(4.47)*

NOTES

NOTES

NOTES

NOTES

GCSE and equivalent levels (£3.50 each)

Maya Angelou
I Know Why the Caged Bird Sings

Jane Austen
Pride and Prejudice

Alan Ayckbourn
Absent Friends

Elizabeth Barrett Browning
Selected Poems

Robert Bolt
A Man for All Seasons

Harold Brighouse
Hobson's Choice

Charlotte Brontë
Jane Eyre

Emily Brontë
Wuthering Heights

Shelagh Delaney
A Taste of Honey

Charles Dickens
David Copperfield

Charles Dickens
Great Expectations

Charles Dickens
Hard Times

Charles Dickens
Oliver Twist

Roddy Doyle
Paddy Clarke Ha Ha Ha

George Eliot
Silas Marner

George Eliot
The Mill on the Floss

William Golding
Lord of the Flies

Oliver Goldsmith
She Stoops To Conquer

Willis Hall
The Long and the Short and the Tall

Thomas Hardy
Far from the Madding Crowd

Thomas Hardy
The Mayor of Casterbridge

Thomas Hardy
Tess of the d'Urbervilles

Thomas Hardy
The Withered Arm and other Wessex Tales

L.P. Hartley
The Go-Between

Seamus Heaney
Selected Poems

Susan Hill
I'm the King of the Castle

Barry Hines
A Kestrel for a Knave

Louise Lawrence
Children of the Dust

Harper Lee
To Kill a Mockingbird

Laurie Lee
Cider with Rosie

Arthur Miller
The Crucible

Arthur Miller
A View from the Bridge

Robert O'Brien
Z for Zachariah

Frank O'Connor
My Oedipus Complex and other stories

George Orwell
Animal Farm

J.B. Priestley
An Inspector Calls

Willy Russell
Educating Rita

Willy Russell
Our Day Out

J.D. Salinger
The Catcher in the Rye

William Shakespeare
Henry IV Part 1

William Shakespeare
Henry V

William Shakespeare
Julius Caesar

William Shakespeare
Macbeth

William Shakespeare
The Merchant of Venice

William Shakespeare
A Midsummer Night's Dream

William Shakespeare
Much Ado About Nothing

William Shakespeare
Romeo and Juliet

William Shakespeare
The Tempest

William Shakespeare
Twelfth Night

George Bernard Shaw
Pygmalion

Mary Shelley
Frankenstein

R.C. Sherriff
Journey's End

Rukshana Smith
Salt on the snow

John Steinbeck
Of Mice and Men

Robert Louis Stevenson
Dr Jekyll and Mr Hyde

Jonathan Swift
Gulliver's Travels

Robert Swindells
Daz 4 Zoe

Mildred D. Taylor
Roll of Thunder, Hear My Cry

Mark Twain
Huckleberry Finn

James Watson
Talking in Whispers

William Wordsworth
Selected Poems

A Choice of Poets

Mystery Stories of the Nineteenth Century including The Signalman

Nineteenth Century Short Stories

Poetry of the First World War

Six Women Poets

Chinua Achebe
Things Fall Apart

Edward Albee
Who's Afraid of Virginia Woolf?

Margaret Atwood
Cat's Eye

Jane Austen
Emma

Jane Austen
Northanger Abbey

Jane Austen
Sense and Sensibility

Samuel Beckett
Waiting for Godot

Robert Browning
Selected Poems

Robert Burns
Selected Poems

Angela Carter
Nights at the Circus

Geoffrey Chaucer
The Merchant's Tale

Geoffrey Chaucer
The Miller's Tale

Geoffrey Chaucer
The Nun's Priest's Tale

Samuel Taylor Coleridge
Selected Poems

Daniel Defoe
Moll Flanders

Daniel Defoe
Robinson Crusoe

Charles Dickens
Bleak House

Charles Dickens
Hard Times

Emily Dickinson
Selected Poems

Carol Ann Duffy
Selected Poems

George Eliot
Middlemarch

T.S. Eliot
The Waste Land

T.S. Eliot
Selected Poems

Henry Fielding
Joseph Andrews

E.M. Forster
Howards End

John Fowles
The French Lieutenant's Woman

Robert Frost
Selected Poems

Elizabeth Gaskell
North and South

Stella Gibbons
Cold Comfort Farm

Graham Greene
Brighton Rock

Thomas Hardy
Jude the Obscure

Thomas Hardy
Selected Poems

Joseph Heller
Catch-22

Homer
The Iliad

Homer
The Odyssey

Gerard Manley Hopkins
Selected Poems

Aldous Huxley
Brave New World

Kazuo Ishiguro
The Remains of the Day

Ben Jonson
The Alchemist

Ben Jonson
Volpone

James Joyce
A Portrait of the Artist as a Young Man

Philip Larkin
Selected Poems

D.H. Lawrence
The Rainbow

D.H. Lawrence
Selected Stories

D.H. Lawrence
Sons and Lovers

D.H. Lawrence
Women in Love

John Milton
Paradise Lost Bks I & II

John Milton
Paradise Lost Bks IV & IX

Thomas More
Utopia

Sean O'Casey
Juno and the Paycock

George Orwell
Nineteen Eighty-four

John Osborne
Look Back in Anger

Wilfred Owen
Selected Poems

Sylvia Plath
Selected Poems

Alexander Pope
Rape of the Lock and other poems

Ruth Prawer Jhabvala
Heat and Dust

Jean Rhys
Wide Sargasso Sea

William Shakespeare
As You Like It

William Shakespeare
Coriolanus

William Shakespeare
Henry IV Pt 1

William Shakespeare
Henry V

William Shakespeare
Julius Caesar

William Shakespeare
Macbeth

William Shakespeare
Measure for Measure

William Shakespeare
A Midsummer Night's Dream

William Shakespeare
Richard II

William Shakespeare
Richard III

William Shakespeare
Sonnets

William Shakespeare
The Taming of the Shrew

York Notes Advanced (£3.99 each)

Margaret Atwood
The Handmaid's Tale

Jane Austen
Mansfield Park

Jane Austen
Persuasion

Jane Austen
Pride and Prejudice

Alan Bennett
Talking Heads

William Blake
*Songs of Innocence and of
Experience*

Charlotte Brontë
Jane Eyre

Emily Brontë
Wuthering Heights

Geoffrey Chaucer
The Franklin's Tale

Geoffrey Chaucer
*General Prologue to the
Canterbury Tales*

Geoffrey Chaucer
*The Wife of Bath's Prologue
and Tale*

Joseph Conrad
Heart of Darkness

Charles Dickens
Great Expectations

John Donne
Selected Poems

George Eliot
The Mill on the Floss

F. Scott Fitzgerald
The Great Gatsby

E.M. Forster
A Passage to India

Brian Friel
Translations

Thomas Hardy
The Mayor of Casterbridge

Thomas Hardy
Tess of the d'Urbervilles

Seamus Heaney
*Selected Poems from Opened
Ground*

Nathaniel Hawthorne
The Scarlet Letter

James Joyce
Dubliners

John Keats
Selected Poems

Christopher Marlowe
Doctor Faustus

Arthur Miller
Death of a Salesman

Toni Morrison
Beloved

William Shakespeare
Antony and Cleopatra

William Shakespeare
As You Like It

William Shakespeare
Hamlet

William Shakespeare
King Lear

William Shakespeare
Measure for Measure

William Shakespeare
The Merchant of Venice

William Shakespeare
Much Ado About Nothing

William Shakespeare
Othello

William Shakespeare
Romeo and Juliet

William Shakespeare
The Tempest

William Shakespeare
The Winter's Tale

Mary Shelley
Frankenstein

Alice Walker
The Color Purple

Oscar Wilde
*The Importance of Being
Earnest*

Tennessee Williams
A Streetcar Named Desire

John Webster
The Duchess of Malfi

W.B. Yeats
Selected Poems

Chinua Achebe
Things Fall Apart

Edward Albee
Who's Afraid of Virginia Woolf?

Margaret Atwood
Cat's Eye

Jane Austen
Emma

Jane Austen
Northanger Abbey

Jane Austen
Sense and Sensibility

Samuel Beckett
Waiting for Godot

Robert Browning
Selected Poems

Robert Burns
Selected Poems

Angela Carter
Nights at the Circus

Geoffrey Chaucer
The Merchant's Tale

Geoffrey Chaucer
The Miller's Tale

Geoffrey Chaucer
The Nun's Priest's Tale

Samuel Taylor Coleridge
Selected Poems

Daniel Defoe
Moll Flanders

Daniel Defoe
Robinson Crusoe

Charles Dickens
Bleak House

Charles Dickens
Hard Times

Emily Dickinson
Selected Poems

Carol Ann Duffy
Selected Poems

George Eliot
Middlemarch

T.S. Eliot
The Waste Land

T.S. Eliot
Selected Poems

Henry Fielding
Joseph Andrews

E.M. Forster
Howards End

John Fowles
The French Lieutenant's Woman

Robert Frost
Selected Poems

Elizabeth Gaskell
North and South

Stella Gibbons
Cold Comfort Farm

Graham Greene
Brighton Rock

Thomas Hardy
Jude the Obscure

Thomas Hardy
Selected Poems

Joseph Heller
Catch-22

Homer
The Iliad

Homer
The Odyssey

Gerard Manley Hopkins
Selected Poems

Aldous Huxley
Brave New World

Kazuo Ishiguro
The Remains of the Day

Ben Jonson
The Alchemist

Ben Jonson
Volpone

James Joyce
A Portrait of the Artist as a Young Man

Philip Larkin
Selected Poems

D.H. Lawrence
The Rainbow

D.H. Lawrence
Selected Stories

D.H. Lawrence
Sons and Lovers

D.H. Lawrence
Women in Love

John Milton

Paradise Lost Bks I & II

John Milton
Paradise Lost Bks IV & IX

Thomas More
Utopia

Sean O'Casey
Juno and the Paycock

George Orwell
Nineteen Eighty-four

John Osborne
Look Back in Anger

Wilfred Owen
Selected Poems

Sylvia Plath
Selected Poems

Alexander Pope
Rape of the Lock and other poems

Ruth Prawer Jhabvala
Heat and Dust

Jean Rhys
Wide Sargasso Sea

William Shakespeare
As You Like It

William Shakespeare
Coriolanus

William Shakespeare
Henry IV Pt 1

William Shakespeare
Henry V

William Shakespeare
Julius Caesar

William Shakespeare
Macbeth

William Shakespeare
Measure for Measure

William Shakespeare
A Midsummer Night's Dream

William Shakespeare
Richard II

William Shakespeare
Richard III

William Shakespeare
Sonnets

William Shakespeare
The Taming of the Shrew

William Shakespeare
Twelfth Night

William Shakespeare
The Winter's Tale

George Bernard Shaw
Arms and the Man

George Bernard Shaw
Saint Joan

Muriel Spark
The Prime of Miss Jean Brodie

John Steinbeck
The Grapes of Wrath

John Steinbeck
The Pearl

Tom Stoppard
Arcadia

Tom Stoppard
Rosencrantz and Guildenstern are Dead

Jonathan Swift
Gulliver's Travels and The Modest Proposal

Alfred, Lord Tennyson
Selected Poems

W.M. Thackeray
Vanity Fair

Virgil
The Aeneid

Edith Wharton
The Age of Innocence

Tennessee Williams
Cat on a Hot Tin Roof

Tennessee Williams
The Glass Menagerie

Virginia Woolf
Mrs Dalloway

Virginia Woolf
To the Lighthouse

William Wordsworth
Selected Poems

Metaphysical Poets

York Notes – the Ultimate Literature Guides

York Notes are recognised as the best literature study guides.
If you have enjoyed using this book and have found it useful, you
can now order others directly from us – simply follow the ordering
instructions below.

HOW TO ORDER

Decide which title(s) you require and then order in one of the following
ways:

Booksellers
All titles available from good bookstores.

By post
List the title(s) you require in the space provided overleaf,
select your method of payment, complete your name and
address details and return your completed order form and
payment to:

Addison Wesley Longman Ltd
PO BOX 88
Harlow
Essex CM19 5SR

By phone
Call our Customer Information Centre on 01279 623923 to
place your order, quoting mail number: HEYN1.

By fax
Complete the order form overleaf, ensuring you fill in your
name and address details and method of payment, and fax it
to us on 01279 414130.

By e-mail
E-mail your order to us on awlhe.orders@awl.co.uk listing
title(s) and quantity required and providing full name and
address details as requested overleaf. Please quote mail
number: HEYN1. Please do not send credit card details by
e-mail.

York Notes Order Form

Titles required:

Quantity	Title/ISBN	Price

Sub total _____

Please add £2.50 postage & packing _____

(*P & P is free for orders over £50*) _____

Total _____

Mail no: HEYN1

Your Name _____

Your Address _____

_____

Postcode _____ Telephone _____

Method of payment

☐ I enclose a cheque or a P/O for £_____ made payable to Addison Wesley Longman Ltd

☐ Please charge my Visa/Access/AMEX/Diners Club card

Number _____ Expiry Date _____

Signature _____ Date _____

(please ensure that the address given above is the same as for your credit card)

Prices and other details are correct at time of going to press but may change without notice. All orders are subject to status.

☐ *Please tick this box if you would like a complete listing of Longman Study Guides (suitable for GCSE and A-level students)*

🌐 York Press

📖 Longman

Addison
Wesley
Longman